JOURNEYING INTO CHEROKEE

JOURNEYING INTO CHEROKEE

Help and Encouragement for Learning
the Cherokee Language

ED FIELDS & MARY RAE

Dog Soldier Press
Ranchos de Taos

Dog Soldier Press
P.O. Box 1782
Ranchos de Taos
New Mexico 87557

ISBN: 979-8-9874524-8-6
Library of Congress Control Number: 2023903714

Cover Art *Climb the Mountain!*: Ed Fields
Interior Drawings: Ed Fields
Book Design and Layout: Mary Rae

TABLE OF CONTENTS

FIGURES

TABLES

EPIGRAPH

'Start and don't stop. What you do after start
determines how fast, how much and
how well you learn.'

—*Ed Fields*

ACKNOWLEDGMENTS

To all who have preserved the Cherokee language in the past and to all who are preserving the Cherokee language now and to all who will be preserving the Cherokee language in the future
GV wado, 'thank you.'

A NOTE ON PHONETICS

In spoken Cherokee, vowels may sometimes be deleted. In this book, deleted vowels are represented as enclosed in parentheses. In addition, spoken Cherokee may include air ('h') sounds not written in the syllabary. This 'h' sound, sometimes called *intrusive h*, is enclosed in forward slashes.

OPENING REMARKS

ED FIELDS

ᏱᏍ *siyo*, 'Hello,' and welcome to *Journeying Into Cherokee*. Some of you have read the subtitle on the front cover, so already know the book is about help and encouragement for learning the Cherokee Language. And maybe some of you looked at the drawing and wondered, 'What do all those things in the drawing represent?' For instance, maybe you noticed the horizontal lines going up the triangle and wondered, 'Why are there lines going up that triangle?' Of course, if you read the title of the cover art on the copyright page then you know the name of the drawing and that the triangle is a mountain, it represents the Cherokee language mountain.

A mountain in real life can look very tall to climb. It can be exciting or intimidating or both to people. When people consider learning the Cherokee language, or are even in the process of learning the Cherokee language, sometimes that Cherokee language mountain may look tall and intimidating. So the lines going up the mountain show it's easy to go up the Cherokee language mountain if you take it one step at a time. That is something to always keep in mind: if you take it a step at a time, it is not hard to do.

It's easier to take a journey or climb a mountain, of course, if you have a guide that points out things to look for and suggests things you can do to make your journey more enjoyable or successful. So this book is not a textbook or lesson book. It is a guide.

I am not a writer, I am not proficient in the English language or in English grammar and composition. Also, I am not a Cherokee linguist. I am just a Cherokee speaker who has taught the language for over 23 years, and I just want to share what I know with you as best as I can.

My co-writer for this guide book is Mary Rae, who I tend to think of as Meli (which is Mary pronounced with Cherokee phonetic sounds Me-li). I know from eight years of Cherokee online classes and two weeks of Cherokee in-person immersion classes and many, many, many hours of phone calls done for collaborations on some Cherokee language projects, that Meli is caring, intelligent, helpful, hard-working, funny, passionate about Cherokee and an amazing person. So you can expect all those things in her chapters on learning the Cherokee language. And since Meli passed both the Cherokee Language Proficiency Test (with a 100%) and passed the Teacher Certification Test (becoming a certified Cherokee language teacher) she has experience of how a second-language learner can study and learn the Cherokee language. So you'll find her chapters helpful.

Briefly, here is a little about what is in the book.

Chapter One, "Why Learn Cherokee?" gives you the very first step of your journey. It tries to help you identify doubts, fears and hindrances you'll face so you can overcome them. It tries to help you create a solid foundation for learning Cherokee. If you don't create a solid foundation, then later you may have trouble or even quit. So even if you've already decided to learn Cherokee, or are years into learning it, Chapter One can still be good to read so that you make sure you get your foundation established and your belief in your goal of learning Cherokee established, or to reinforce them both.

Chapter Two, "Stepping Onto the Path," is by Meli who tells you how studying Cherokee changed her life. She lists some benefits of learning Cherokee. She dispels some harmful language-learning myths and negative statements that hinder you from learning. She gives tips for success in learning Cherokee. Meli uses her own personal experience as a second-language learner of the Cherokee language to help you create your solid foundation for learning Cherokee so you can have a successful journey.

Chapter Three, "Where to Start?" is about where from an actual place perspective—online and in-person classes and programs out there to learn Cherokee. It gives a tip for figuring out where you want to start. It talks of some ways of finding these classes, programs and ways of learning Cherokee. It also covers some things you can do at home to help yourself learn Cherokee. It touches on what it takes to learn to be fluent, and why it is important to make sure you are getting real Cherokee meanings and worldview.

Chapter Four, "If I Can Learn, So Can You," is about where to start too, but Meli looks at the topic as in where in the process of learning the language do you start—with syllabary or verbs or something else. She shares with you how she went about beginning to learn, how to approach problems that arise in your Cherokee language learning journey so you can overcome them, and how to learn so that you can understand deeply. She gives you practical suggestions that you can actually do to begin learning and to find yourself learning Cherokee daily.

Chapter Five, "How is Cherokee Different From English?" is about some of the differences between the Cherokee and English languages that people have asked me about or commented on over the years. But it is also about some of the similarities between the Cherokee and English languages. It also touches upon the Cherokee syllabary, the Six Grandpas and Their Family Members, sounds, dialects, whether one should learn to read and write with phonetics or syllabary, word length and seeks to help you realize that with time and practice you can learn the Cherokee language.

Chapter Six, "Making Friends With Cherokee Verbs," is by Meli who touches upon the differences between the English and Cherokee languages, and she gives tips on how to find words in the Cherokee dictionary since it's not the same as using an English dictionary. Meli explains the various parts of the Cherokee verb and helps you begin to actually be able to use Cherokee verbs. She also gives you tips you can do to bring yourself closer to thinking in Cherokee. Meli explains things in ways that are easy to understand, so you will be able to use them in your journey into the Cherokee language from day one of reading her chapters.

Chapter Seven, "Which Meaning?" is about some Cherokee meanings (I say 'some' because I cannot include all meanings in one chapter), and I try to illustrate some Cherokee verb meanings for you like I would if you were in online classes with me. Chapter Seven also includes some information that will help you when you translate, or when you ask someone to translate, something from English into Cherokee or from Cherokee into English. It also lists some resources you can use to find Cherokee words used in context so you can get their real Cherokee meaning for when you are learning and translating.

Chapter Eight, "From One Language to Another," discusses translating too as Meli explains more about the differences between the Cherokee and English languages as well as explains the Cherokee classificatory verb, and she gives tips for understanding how to translate English-into-Cherokee and Cherokee-into-English. She details her own learning journey of how she learned. She shares an important discovery she made along her Cherokee language journey when she was translating a song into the Cherokee language and reveals what resources she used and steps she took to do that translation. She gives a helpful tip on how to experience the Cherokee words from not outside but inside the Cherokee world.

Chapter Nine, "Translation in Action," is a translation that Meli and I did by phone. We dual-recorded the entire process we took of translating an English epigraph into Cherokee. Then the recordings were transcribed into a transcript that shows what part I say and what part Meli says. And then the very long transcript was edited to fit into the chapter. I added a sort of running commentary to my part of the transcript to try to show you my thoughts and what was going on during the translation process. If you find my commentary distracting or want to ignore it, then don't read the parts in parentheses, as that is the commentary. We hope this chapter helps you see the translation process in action and know how the translating process works (at least how it works for Meli and me).

"Concluding Thoughts" mentions how this book came about. And it shares with you my hopes and wishes.

"Frequently Asked Questions" covers many questions that students and others have asked over the years. Meli or I answer them one by one. The topics covered are in an easy-to-find format as they are grouped under headings.

"Resources" are several pages that list Cherokee materials you'll find useful and helpful for learning the Cherokee language. These are covered in an easy-to-find format as they too are grouped under headings. There is also a link to learningcherokee.com where more resources are listed.

"Notes" are the notes on Meli's chapters.

"Bibliography" lists the resources Meli used for her chapters.

Of course, my brief descriptions here don't cover everything in the chapters. It's hard to include everything Meli and I talk about in each chapter. I can't list each story we told, or picture I drew, or Figure/Table from Meli, or Cherokee word given and, of course, there's humor (at least we hope there's humor). These are just brief descriptions that I hope help you see what the chapters are sort of like.

Also, you'll notice as you read the chapters that when Meli and I introduce a Cherokee word for the first time that we use syllabary followed by phonetics followed by English meaning (like with ᏏᏲ *siyo*, 'Hello' above). If I had to choose between using only the syllabary along with the English meaning or only the phonetics along with the English meaning to write this, I would have chosen to use the syllabary as that is the written form of Cherokee. But I am not a second-language learner, so all three are used.

This using of all three (syllabary, phonetics, 'English meaning') also meant that when the Cherokee word was introduced and later repeated, then for the repeat either all three would have to be used again or only the syllabary or only the phonetics. Most readers will not be able to read syllabary, and yet to give you only phonetics seemed wrong, after all, how are you going to learn to read syllabary if we don't use syllabary? So all three (syllabary, phonetics, 'English meaning') are used. I realize this may seem repetitive and take up space, but to me helping you learn the Cherokee language is worth being repetitive and taking up a little space.

I will now address some other things. You will probably have heard or read that the Cherokee language is in danger of dying in our lifetimes. Sometimes when people hear or read that, people may feel guilty because they don't have enough time or energy or money or whatever to learn Cherokee the way they want. But there are always some things, even little things, that we each can do.

And sometimes, because they hear or read that the language is dying, people feel as if they're pressured or some other negative. But please know that Meli and I (and even no one I know) wants you to feel pressured or some other negative. The facts about the language are just that, facts, and they have to be looked at and considered. After all, how can people change the facts if they don't know the facts? Facts are not like truth. Truth cannot be changed. But facts can be changed. Facts can change with new knowledge or with proof-giving actions that call for the wrong information to be corrected. Negative facts can be changed to positive facts. So if you are feeling pressured or negative then know that we do not want you to feel that way.

But also know that if you continue to feel that way, then maybe it is your own heart asking you to do something to help save the language. Of course, only you can know if it is your heart. Meli and I cannot know that. But if it is your heart, then you can take that pressure or negative feeling and turn it into a positive by doing something positive or useful.

For myself, I have decided to try to be positive about it all, including to take positive actions. Yes, I have to face reality. The facts state that fewer than 2,000 Cherokee first-language speakers remain, and there will be fewer and fewer each year. Some publications or people will probably do yearly countdowns until the number gets pretty low or, maybe (though hopefully not) even reaches zero. My part is to try to do what I can to bring the numbers up. That means doing two things. One thing to do is to share the Cherokee language so it gets spoken and taught by adults, teens and children in Cherokee homes again, as this will also help the very young children and babies hear it and learn it in Cherokee homes again too, so that the circle continues and hopefully grows. And the other thing to do is share the Cherokee language so it gets spoken and taught by second-language learners of all ages so that they too will learn it and pass it on to others.

Several years ago I told online Cherokee language students that I wanted Cherokee to be spoken around the world. With technology and the help of all of you it has a chance to do that. It has a chance to live, to flourish and to thrive. It can sometimes seem an uphill climb, but it is worth doing.

I hope you enjoy your journey into the Cherokee language. And that this book helps you.

ᎤᏩ *wado,* 'Thank you.'

—Ed

JOURNEYING INTO CHEROKEE

CHAPTER ONE

Why Learn Cherokee?

ED FIELDS

Ꮟ Ꭺ *siyo*, 'Hello,' I'm glad you're here, I've never written a book for publication before and English is not my first language. I'm a little nervous, not as much as the first time I taught online class though. Then, it felt like hundreds of eyes watching me but I couldn't see them and I was like Elvis Presley—I was shaking so bad that day that I was 'all shook up.'

It's funny now, looking back, but at the time it was scary. Sometimes I still get a little bit nervous teaching online classes, but knowing the students are there wanting to learn helps. Knowing that some of my students are here too helps. And that others are here, interested in wanting to learn the Cherokee language and wanting to help the Cherokee language survive and grow and thrive helps me to write this. So ᎬᏩ *wado*, 'thank you' for being here and helping me.

For those of you who don't know me I guess I should tell you a little about myself. I was born into the Cherokee language, born into the Cherokee worldview. That is, my parents were Cherokee and fluent in the Cherokee language. I grew up in a Cherokee-speaking home viewing the world and living in the world the way a Cherokee views and lives in it.

When I reached the age of a first-grader, I had to go to school. It was a two-room schoolhouse and the rooms were the same size, but the room for the older children was called the 'big room' and the room for the younger children was called the 'little room.' The 'big room' had the fourth through eighth graders and the 'little room' had the first through third graders. The school had around twenty children and two teachers. One teacher taught the 'big kids' and one taught the 'little kids.' I was a 'little kid' so went to the 'little room' with the teacher for 'little kids.' She did not punish me or try to make me stop speaking my Cherokee language. She spoke English because that was her language and the only one she knew and school subjects were in English and I did not understand her or the school subjects either.

I don't think I can put into words what it felt like to be away from my familiar home and my loving Cherokee parents and my Cherokee world and Cherokee worldview for all day long, day after day, five days a week in a non-Cherokee world. I cannot say it was paralyzingly scary because I did function, but school was a foreign place where a very confusing language was spoken and I did not understand that language. And that language seemed hard to understand.

There were a few other Cherokee students in the 'little room' and the teacher assigned a Cherokee girl who spoke Cherokee and English to help me but the girl did not. Instead she stayed around the girls. So the teacher gave me coloring books and crayons and pencils and papers and I drew a lot and colored a lot. She interacted with the other children who spoke English and I was on my own to draw and color. She did read schoolbooks to the class but I did not understand what she was reading. She asked me questions but I did not understand and could not answer. So I was taken out of the group and left in a spot by myself away from her and the other children.

The same teacher taught second grade and it was basically the same thing. I was left to my own resources. Which meant I spent a lot of time just thinking or drawing or wishing I was at the creek, wishing I was playing with my dogs or just wishing I was home. At least there were recesses and lunch, and that helped (the food was *really* good, home-cooking, and I especially remember the macaroni and cheese, coleslaw and chocolate pudding as I had never had them before).

In the third grade it was still the same teacher but now I could understand a *little* bit more of English because English was everywhere. It was at school, at the stores, in town—everywhere. And picking up a *little* bit more English meant I was able to participate in class a *little* bit more. She brought me back into the group whenever I could fit in, when I could do the work or answer questions, but mainly I did not because I did not understand. She tried to involve me in things but I just could not answer because I did not know the correct words to say to respond. Since I could not understand most of the schoolbooks and could not keep up with the other children she again gave me pencils and papers and crayons and coloring books. I could not understand her enough and she could not understand me enough to really communicate. That meant that most times I was left either not understanding or I had to try to figure things out for myself.

For instance, I figured out that when someone in English says 'cat' they mean ᏪᏌ *wesa*. But this rule was also not always so. I remember one day the children were excited, they said 'there is a cat outside!' and I looked outside expecting to see a cat and all I saw was a big machine. I wondered, how is that a ᏪᏌ *wesa?* (See Figure 1.1)

Over time I learned it was a brand name and people just shortened it down and called the heavy machines that. Another time she had the group of children in a circle and I was in the back of the group. The students real close could see the pictures in the book, but I could not, and she was reading the book to the class and said the word 'catapult' and the children called it that too and I wondered what kind of 'cat' was a 'catapult,' but later when I looked in the book there was no 'cat.' I learned that English had lots of those and other kinds of confusing and hard to understand things. But I did begin to pick up a little English—because it's hard to not pick up a language when you're immersed in it.

Figure 1.1. Cats and Road Grader

In the fourth grade I had a different teacher. He concentrated more on math with us. And I could understand math more since it was numbers and not English. I learned well enough that I could help other students work out math problems. It felt good to understand a school subject and help others.

I did better in fifth grade. I could speak English better and talk in English with the other children, that is, most of the times I could understand them and if I didn't I could say 'huh?' and they could understand me. Except that I could not put a map together of the United States. I had to search for the names of the states, but I did not even know the names. They were written in English and even though I could read a little English I could not read them. And it wouldn't have done me any good because I had never heard of the names and did not know where to put them on a map. The other students all did good. But I could not do it. The teacher did not give me a grade for that project because I could not do it.

It would not be until about sixth grade that I understood enough English to be able to start helping my parents, elders and others by interpreting. It felt good to be able to help.

As the years went by I graduated grade-school, high-school, and entered university. Through all those years I interpreted for those who needed it and was glad I could help. And I wanted to become a teacher and teach art to elementary students and put some Cherokee words into the lessons every day, even if teaching Cherokee wasn't required. But during my university years I was drafted into military service and later sent overseas to the war.

After coming back, it was rough for a while. Eventually I decided to go back to university. But I did not understand how the higher education system worked. I do not remember anyone explaining it. Maybe they expected me to know, but I didn't. So I simply took classes. I took a lot of art classes because they were fun. After the war, some of the other classes were depressing. And some were hard to get through, especially if they required more English. (Rita, my wife, later pointed out I only started learning to speak a *little* English in third grade and reading and writing in fifth or six, so I was trying to do university level English without a full twelve years of English learning.) Because I just took classes and then they counted them up somehow and determined what my major and minors were, I did not graduate with a teaching degree. I found that my degrees turned out to be a B.A. in Art and minors in Psychology and Sociology.

And I went to work at a canning factory, then at chicken plants, then back to the canning factory where I worked my way up to supervisor, and when the canning department went out I was put into the freezer—just a little joke—I was put in the frozen foods department. Then we moved and I got a job glazing tile and later also designing tile. When the tile company closed its doors in the late 1980s, I went to work at a nursing home. But I still wanted to teach, so I decided to go back to university. I took night classes while continuing to work days at the nursing home.

I was doing okay in classes, usually I made B's although sometimes I made A's and C's. And because I had gone to university before, they said I now only had one or two semesters to go and I would graduate as a teacher. It was a good feeling, working towards my dream and watching it come closer and closer to coming true.

But then the higher education rules changed. They said that my old grades before the war up to current grades would all be totaled together. And I had some bad grades. This totaling together dropped my grade point average too far. I was told that I would have to make straight A's for two years in a row in order to be able to get my teaching degree. I had never been able to make straight A's, so making straight A's two years in a row seemed impossible. But I asked university professors and people who worked in higher-education who knew what my grades were and what they thought I could do, and they told me I couldn't do it. And there was still the debt factor. Why take on more debt for something that was impossible, especially when those in the know knew I couldn't do it?

I put aside my dream of getting a university teaching degree, being a state certified teacher and teaching, and left university.

This was not easy. Knowing my disappointment and discouragement, Rita tried to help me figure out ways to still get my dream. 'Go to an out-of-state university,' she said, 'they might still have the old GPA rules that don't mix very old grades with new grades, then you can still become a teacher in one or two semesters and not two years.' But I wouldn't do this. There was no guarantee. And it would be just racking up more debt that would hurt us in the long run. After that, she tried again, 'If you volunteer as a tutor for children for enough years then maybe you could get paid to do that.' But, again, I would not do this. Tutoring was volunteer with no pay and I had bills to pay and college loans to pay, and even if I did it for years there was no guarantee they would hire me. Finally she saw that I was just not going to try any of those things and was going to move on to something else, so she told me that if teaching was what ᎤᏁᎳᏅᎯ *Unetlanvhi*, 'Creator, God' wanted me to do, then someday I would teach, that ᎤᏁᎳᏅᎯ *Unetlanvhi*, 'Creator, God' would work it out. And to this I could agree.

I had to look around for a better paying job because now I also had college loans to pay off. I found work as a Home Health Aide. I enjoyed helping people and I got to share Cherokee stories, Cherokee words and Cherokee nature lore with people when I went to their homes to help them. They really enjoyed that. And so did I. I liked making them laugh, smile and feel good. I also helped Cherokee elders, who were not at home in the English language, and their nurses, who could not speak Cherokee, by acting as interpreter for them.

During this time I took the Cherokee Nation Teacher's Certification Program under Durbin Feeling. Durbin was the teacher and this program required me to also teach Cherokee one year, so I worked in Home Health during the day and taught a Cherokee evening class for free a little over one year, and became a certified Cherokee language teacher. There were no jobs for teaching Cherokee though, so I stayed in the Home Health industry.

Then the Home Health industry changed. There was a big pay drop, and workers were having to get hired by three or four different companies doing part-time jobs in two, three, four different counties. I got four part-time jobs and was driving hundreds of miles a day all over four counties to clients' homes. But you couldn't make a living. So I also took on a full-time nurse aide job from late night to early morning. Even then, I couldn't make the pay that I had been making. Times got real rough for my family and me, and it looked as if they'd always be so, or maybe even worse.

Then Rita showed me a newspaper ad about job positions in the Cherokee Nation Cultural Resource Center. She said that I should put in an application. I said, 'I'm not qualified or equipped for any of those.' She said even if I was not that ᎤᏁᎳᏅᎯ *Unetlanvhi*, 'Creator, God' would help me and equip me. But I said, 'I can't do them.' She said that we'd pray and trust ᎤᏁᎳᏅᎯ *Unetlanvhi*,

'Creator, God.' That was fine with me. But I said, 'I don't know which to apply for.' She said, 'All of them.' Then she said we'd let ᎤᏁᏛᎢ *Unetlanvhi*, 'Creator, God' make the decision of which job I'd get.

So I applied for all the jobs. And we continued to pray, trust ᎤᏁᏛᎢ *Unetlanvhi*, 'Creator, God' and be thankful for the help of ᎤᏁᏛᎢ *Unetlanvhi*, 'Creator, God' while we waited for the time of my job interview to arrive.

The time arrived. The lady who interviewed me was nice. She didn't tell me that I was not qualified for any of the positions, she just told me what each position was like and the work required and after each description would ask me if I thought I would like that type of work. I decided that I liked the position of Cherokee language instructor best. And I was hired on a trial-basis, part-time. Eventually my boss asked me if I wanted to go full-time. I said yes and began working full time.

When I came in for the interview I could speak Cherokee, and my university courses in education—including Loretta Shade's Cherokee class and teaching a group in her class one semester—and my past work history as Cherokee interpreter, my Cherokee Language course work under Durbin Feeling, teaching Cherokee for little over one year and being a certified Cherokee language teacher, all that helped. ᎤᏁᏛᎢ *Unetlanvhi*, 'Creator, God' didn't let any of that go to waste.

I have now been working for the Cherokee Nation since 2000 and have been a Cherokee National Treasure in the language since 2010. I teach the online Cherokee language classes and the in-person Cherokee immersion classes. And when not doing those, I'm preparing materials or new lessons for them and I sometimes help out in interpreting or storytelling or cultural camps or other tasks of the Language Department. I'm not a state certified teacher. I'm listed as a Cherokee instructor. It was my online students who began to call me 'Teacher Ed' or 'ᏗᏕᏲᎲᏍᎩ *dideyohvsgi* Ed.' My students are great people.

You may be reading all this and wondering 'why is he telling me all these things' or 'what has this to do with me and learning Cherokee' or even thinking some other thing. I wanted to tell you these things for you to be able to know me a little, but also to hopefully help you see that life does not always go in a straight line. Sometimes it is convoluted, like a path that goes around trees and boulders and circles cliffs and goes a long way to find a place to cross a river and then goes around other obstacles but it always goes onward to its destination. Maybe like me, you had a dream too. Maybe your dream was to learn Cherokee and things interfered. It's not too late to pick up that dream and breathe new life into it. Or maybe you have that dream now, to learn Cherokee or be able to help or work in the Cherokee language in some way, and that dream is going about in a convoluted way and you are tempted to give up. Don't give up. Someday you will reach the destination and be able to look back at the trees, boulders, cliffs, rivers and such that were in your way. You will be able to see the convoluted journey. Right now, it cannot be seen in its entirety. But journey onward and it will be.

Or maybe, like me, you heard negative news or were told that you do not have what it takes to do it and you are discouraged, sad, tempted to give up and walk away. I want you to know that you do have what it takes to learn Cherokee. Whether you have time and resources to learn a lot or whether you have very little time and resources and must walk the journey just a little bit at a time. You can do it. Every little bit helps. And someday you can look back and see the journey that you took.

In fact, let me share with you some things that will help you as you go forward in your Cherokee language journey.

Years ago, around the 1980s and even into the 1990s, people were saying things like 'the experts say do not teach your child Cherokee because you will hurt them.' They said 'if you teach your child Cherokee they won't be able to learn English good enough, this will hurt them in school, hurt them in jobs, hurt them in life.'

These sayings, and others like them, influenced many parents, grandparents and relatives to not teach their children their Cherokee language, because they didn't want to hurt the children in any way. So many Cherokee children were not taught their native language.

Then, several years after that, people began to say things like 'the experts say that teaching a child a second language helps them. It does not hurt them.' And 'learning a second language helps your child to learn other languages too.' And 'learning a second language helps your child be able to solve problems in more than one way, it trains their brains to be able to come at something from different angles, to be creative problem-solvers.' But the damage of the first statement, with its wrong information, had been done. It gave doubt and fear a big helping hand to stop the Cherokee people from teaching their children their native language. It hindered the growth and thriving of the Cherokee language.

And even after the second saying of the experts, when the new statement was that by teaching your child a second language you were helping them, they didn't say to teach them the Cherokee language. It was always to teach them other languages, what they call the 'romance' languages. Which made the second statement, that teaching a child a second language did not hurt them, not as helpful to the growth and thriving of the Cherokee language as it could have been.

During the beginning years of Cherokee online classes, a different statement began to be heard. They said 'if you're not born into a Cherokee home where Cherokee is spoken then you won't be able to learn it.' And even when I said that isn't so, that you can learn regardless, many did not believe. Then along comes Patrick Del Percio. He was about 14. He didn't live in Cherokee country around speakers, in fact, he lived several states away. He wasn't born into a Cherokee speaking home. He didn't grow up in a Cherokee speaking home. And he learns the Cherokee language. He learns it so well that Cherokee elders and Patrick can converse and understand each other. He learns it so well the elders say to me 'he speaks like a Cherokee, he speaks fluent.' And over time he learned it so well that he went on to teach the Cherokee language at a university.

You would think this would be a great inspiration, that people could see that it was possible to learn the Cherokee language even if you weren't born into a Cherokee home in Cherokee country. But then a new statement came along.

They began to say 'well, a *young* person can learn Cherokee, but an adult can't learn it.' And even when I refuted that, many didn't believe. And then along comes Mary Rae. She didn't live in Cherokee country around speakers, in fact, she lived several states away. She wasn't born into a Cherokee speaking home. She didn't grow up in a Cherokee speaking home. She wasn't in her teens. In fact, she was retired. And she learns Cherokee. She learns it so well she passes the proficiency test. She learns it so well she passes the Cherokee Teacher Certification Test and amazes the Cherokee speaker giving the test. She learns it so well she can now teach the Cherokee language if she wants.

I still hear variants of these statements of wrong information that try to cause fears and doubts to stop people from even trying to start. And I hear other statements that try to stop learners along their journey of learning the Cherokee language.

Sometimes they say 'I don't have anyone at home to talk Cherokee with so I can't learn Cherokee' and I say 'neither did Patrick Del Percio, neither did Mary Rae but they learned it, it can be done.' Sometimes they say 'Cherokee is too hard, too difficult to learn' and I say 'look at English, look how many definitions there are for one word. Look at the word 'bear.' I counted the definitions in a dictionary once for the word 'bear' and do you know how many there were? There were around forty definitions for the word 'bear.' It had definitions for it as a noun, as an intransitive verb, as a transitive verb, as an adjective, as an idiom and so on. Almost forty definitions for the one word 'bear.' But in Cherokee it's not like that. In Cherokee you'd say ᏯᎾ *yona* for 'bear.' Cherokee is easier.

And in English you have twenty-six letters that make sounds that you then have to put together to form syllables. But in Cherokee the syllables are already put together for you. Cherokee is easier.

The truth is, there will always be statements of wrong information that try to get you to fear starting to learn the Cherokee language or to try to stop you along the journey. There will always be statements of wrong information to try to get you to doubt that you can learn the Cherokee language. But notice the little word 'try'—that little word tells you that the choice is up to you, you can accept the statements of wrong information and choose to believe the fears and doubts and let them hinder or stop you or you can choose to not accept them and choose to walk step-by-step forward into your Cherokee language journey.

The truth of the matter is that you can learn the Cherokee language. You can learn a little, you can learn a medium amount or you can learn a lot. How fast and how much and how well you learn depends on you. Just like with Patrick, it depended on him and what he chose to do. Just like with Mary Rae, it depended on her and what she chose to do.

Besides the statements of wrong information that try to instill fear and doubt to stop you, there are other statements that try to hinder you. Some hindering statement you might hear is 'do not speak Cherokee unless you can pronounce it perfectly' or 'do not speak unless you can say it correctly.' No one holds English learners to that standard. Learners of English are allowed to grow into learning the language, if they make mistakes they are told they will learn as they go along. But for some reason with Cherokee it is different. I have heard people say this to learners and the learners be discouraged or even afraid they are offending those they respect and honor and so they think they should not speak unless they can do it perfectly or correctly. But this is not the way, one should be allowed to grow, to progress. One should not be made to fear, to be so rigid they cannot breathe. Growing up in the Cherokee world, in the Cherokee language, I do not know of one Cherokee who told another person to not speak unless they did it perfectly, correctly. This was not the Cherokee way. We were always respectful and honored others but we also knew there would be mistakes and we encouraged learning and growth. They knew they would learn. My parents would always say GƟSⳚ⳨ ꭰƟꞨᏈꭺ *yunaduliha yanadeloqua*, 'if they want to they will learn.'

A learner needs to be aware of hindering statements and wrong information and know them for what they are and stand against them in their minds and hearts and lives. If you live by them you will be hindered or even stopped in your learning.

It is a wonderful thing to see people do what is needed to learn. Such joy they have when they first understand a native speaker. Such joy they have when they first begin to be able to communicate back and forth with a native speaker. That joy can be yours too.

Each learner will face statements of wrong information, fear, doubt, hindrances and such and have to overcome them or be overcome by them. So it is best you know of them ahead of time. Then you can be prepared. Then you can shrug them off like ꭰꝞꝺ *kawona*, 'duck' does water from its back. And you can go forward, learning the Cherokee language. (See Figure 1.2).

Figure 1.2. Duck

Another statement that tries to stop people from even starting is that they've heard that 'learning Cherokee is too hard' so they fear they cannot learn it, they doubt they can learn it, that people will ridicule them or that they themselves will think badly of themselves. But look at it like this. Some say the Cherokee language is in danger of dying, that maybe one or two generations is all that is left and then it is dead. Even if you only learn a little and can pass that on you would be a help to the survival of the Cherokee language.

Also, whether you become fluent or whether you only learn a little, you can inspire someone else to learn. And that helps too. Everyone who wants to help is needed. Who knows, maybe your mail carrier will see a postcard that you wrote ᏏᏲ ᏙᎯᏧ *siyo tohitsu*, 'hello, how are you' on and get interested in learning the language. Or a neighbor, co-worker, friend, relative, cashier or someone else may hear that you are learning the Cherokee language and they themselves get inspired to join in the effort to save the language, to grow the language and help it thrive.

You don't know what you can do until you set about it and you don't know everyone you will influence. Always remember, even little steps forward along the journey make a big difference when a language needs help to survive. You can be part of an important, language-saving, very needed group of people who are seeking to preserve, grow and help the Cherokee language thrive.

But you are going to have to face the fact that you're going to hear wrong information statements that try to cause doubts and fears at the beginning of your Cherokee language journey and all along the way of it and even perhaps when you are fluent. Learn to take a look at the statements you hear as well as those that you're saying to yourself. Look at them from every angle. Ask yourself, are they really the truth? Most times they're wrong information that causes fears and doubts to stop you from starting or even to make you give up and quit. If you can't refute them, ask someone who has been along the journey before you. Or simply carry on going forward regardless of the statements of wrong information, doubts, fears.

I have heard it said that you only fail when you quit, until then you're still trying and still going forward in whatever size steps you take.

I have also heard it said that true courage is doing something even when you're afraid. And many times once you begin you find that all the fears and doubts weren't real. But you'll not know until you step out and begin to walk on your journey into learning the Cherokee language.

When we put aside statements of wrong information that instill fears and doubts, when we put aside hindering statements that harm and hurt, when we help build instead of ridicule or destroy, when we take each other's hand and help each other along the journey—what great things can be done. And what great lives are lived.

If you're of Cherokee descent, learning the Cherokee language gives you a connection with your ancestors. Your ancestors spoke Cherokee. Imagine you speaking the language Sequoyah and your great-great-great grandfather or grandmother or your parents and so on spoke. Hearing the language becomes something special which cannot be put into words but is felt clear to your heart and throughout all your being. And when you not only hear but understand, that is something precious. And when you begin to speak Cherokee, that is something worth more than you can put into words.

If you're not of Cherokee descent, remember that many nationalities lived among and traveled among and traded with and spoke with the Cherokee people and they would have heard Cherokee spoken. British people, American people, the French, Spanish, Germans and other nationalities. Maybe your ancestor was from one of the nationalities who heard Cherokee and even learned Cherokee enough to speak some or even be fluent in Cherokee in their living among and traveling among and trading with the Cherokee people.

And when you think of the near destruction of the Cherokee people and language, when you think of all the work our Cherokee ancestors and good people of other nationalities did together, all the time, effort, suffering and sacrificing while trying to save the Cherokee people and the Cherokee language—how can we let all that good work and sacrifice pass away without seeking to try, in whatever way we can and whatever amount we can, to save the Cherokee language.

Today there are people from different nationalities who are interested in saving and growing and helping the Cherokee language to thrive. Cherokee people long have known that by ᏎᏍᎩ *gadugi,* 'working together' we can do great things.

I hope you decide to take the journey of learning the Cherokee language. And I hope the basic information Meli (Mary) and I share with you in the space limits of this book helps you as you take your journey into learning the Cherokee language. ᎠᏪ *wado,* 'Thank you.'

CHAPTER TWO

Stepping Onto the Path

MARY RAE

In 2014, I embarked upon a journey that would change my life. I began online Cherokee classes with Ed Fields. I've never been accused of being overly dramatic. Not to my face, at least. But I admit that my sweeping statement might seem a little suspect. Studying Cherokee changed my life? Yet, it is true.

Since I was a child, I've felt deeply about music, art, reading and writing. One might guess that I've left at least some of those things behind to make room for the Cherokee language. It takes time to learn a language, and no one can do everything. But I have left nothing behind. Instead, all my interests are now connected to Cherokee. I've explored singing in Cherokee and I've recorded Cherokee hymns; I've used art and music in videos about the language; I've written stories from memories of my childhood in Cherokee; and I've read old texts written in the language. The language has become part of me.

Cherokee has also changed my way of looking at everything around me. Every language reflects a culture's unique way of viewing the world. Through the lens of Cherokee, I see a world more precisely drawn and more richly painted. I often find myself thinking of situations where Cherokee fits better than English. Where I can describe things more directly. More elegantly.

I have also been changed by the wonderful people I have met because of studying Cherokee. I've made many friends who are walking along the same path and who share my joy in the language. Through Cherokee classes, I've been in touch with people from all over the United States, as well as other countries such as Belgium, Germany, Serbia and Italy. Our backgrounds are different, yet we all are brought together by our interest in learning the language. Yes, Cherokee has changed my life.

How did I begin along this road to learning Cherokee? I had been wanting to learn the language for years, but hadn't known where to start. It's hard for me to imagine now that I grew up in a time with no Internet. I might just as well say I lived in an entirely different universe. It almost seems that way now. If I wanted to learn something when I was young, I turned to books. I enjoyed reading and, as the youngest of seven, I found myself surrounded by a ready-made library accumulated by my siblings and parents. There were books about birds, trains, stamps, poetry, art, science, literature, archaeology, electronics and much more. But there were no books on the Cherokee language. Such were the limitations of life before the Internet.

If someone had told me when I was in high-school that one day I would be using a computer I would have laughed. Computers took up entire rooms back then, and held no interest for me. But changes sneak up on people gradually over time, and what once seemed outlandish becomes an everyday reality. There have been so many changes I never could have foreseen. I saw the beautiful woods where I grew up cut down to make way for a shopping center, and the house where I grew up replaced by a parking lot. I saw remote controls, calculators and eventually computers become commonplace. By 2014, I wasn't the least bit surprised that using a computer had become second-nature to me. One day it dawned on me that I might find information online about learning Cherokee.

When I came across the Cherokee Nation's online classes I was overjoyed. Finally, I had found a way to begin.

Entering Ed Fields' online class was like stepping into a different world. First, there was the fascinating writing system called the syllabary, instead of an alphabet. The Cherokee syllabary consists of eighty-six characters, many of which are very unusual looking, though some resemble English letters. Eighty-six? Just a little bit daunting. I was relieved that no one was expected to learn them all right away, but the characters seemed to be circling overhead until I gave them my attention. And from the first day, I learned that I had to shift my thinking out of the English language, where I'd been lounging around quite comfortably for years, and into the great unknown of the Cherokee language, where words paint pictures in detail unimagined in English. Cherokee definitely got my attention. No more lounging around.

I didn't know it at the time, but I was very fortunate to have started in Ed Fields' class. It is an amazing experience to learn from someone like Ed, who teaches from inside the language, showing students how to see things as a native speaker sees them, rather than from an English point of view. This was going to be a challenge, I realized. I was intrigued.

I didn't expect that learning Cherokee would be easy. But I didn't expect it would be hard either. In fact, I had no preconceived idea what it would be like to study Cherokee. I have since learned that most people consider Cherokee to be a very difficult language to learn.

In the 1970s, classifications were devised by the Foreign Service Institute and other government agencies to assess how long it would take for an English speaker to reach an advanced level of proficiency in another language. Languages which are most similar to English, such as Spanish, French and Dutch, predictably fall into the Class I category. Cherokee, although not officially ranked, is thought by most to fit the criteria for a Class IV language, along with languages such as Chinese, Korean, Japanese and Arabic. This means that it is considered to be among the most difficult languages for native speakers of English to master.

It is true that there is nothing in the Cherokee language that a new student can sail through. Someone studying Spanish, a Class I language, can progress at a much more rapid rate than someone learning Cherokee. First of all, English and Spanish use the same alphabet and share Latin roots. There are many words in Spanish that look similar to English, and quite a few have the same exact spelling, just with different pronunciations. Here are a few examples, with the Spanish words on the left and English on the right:

excelente / excellent
bicicleta / bicycle
perfecto / perfect
durable / durable
nación / nation
contacto / contact
original /original
simple / simple
ficción / fiction
numeroso / numerous
doctor / doctor
rosa / rose
social / social
diccionario / dictionary

It's easy to see that an English speaker can very quickly pick up new vocabulary in Spanish. In fact, if you were tested on the meanings of the Spanish words you just read, I'm pretty sure you would get them all correct.

Cherokee, on the other hand, has no words similar to English words, except for a handful of recently added sound-a-likes, so new learners have nothing familiar to give them a leg up. Look again at the word 'doctor' from the list. It is spelled exactly the same in Spanish as in English. In Cherokee, 'doctor' would be spelled DSѲSꙀ *aganag(a)ti*. A new student of Cherokee would not find anything familiar that would help them remember the meaning of this word. Cherokee may take longer to learn, but if you are motivated to learn, you won't regret the time you spend studying Cherokee.

There is also the question of finding available resources in Cherokee. Book stores have materials in many languages to help a beginner get started. Internet resources are also plentiful for languages from Italian to Japanese, and you can find countless grammar books and courses. There are even opportunities to have conversations with native speakers online in many languages such as Korean and French. I wish I could say all the same resources were available for Cherokee, but it just isn't so. It's important to remember that those other languages have millions of native speakers while the population of native Cherokee speakers is extremely small. There is good news, however. Many dedicated people are working every day to create more resources and learning materials for Cherokee. You will find an extensive list of resources at the end of this book.

The Cherokee language can seem formidable at first, even if you are highly motivated. About half-way through my first session of online classes with Ed Fields, I started to catch a glimmer of just how involved the language could be. It was like a scary movie where you suddenly see a shadow behind the curtain, and you just know it's going to be bad. In this case, the menace came from verbs so complex I didn't even know how to look them up in the dictionary. Gives me chills just to think about it.

To my relief, I figured out pretty quickly that Cherokee was not that frightening after all. It was challenging enough to keep me on my toes, but not impossible. The fact that I have a B.A. in Spanish and also studied Russian helped me. Having studied languages before may seem like a tremendous advantage, and it was, but not for the reason most people may think. Spanish and Russian have almost nothing in common with Cherokee, and nothing about either language helped me to think in Cherokee. What did help me, though, was that I had learned that all languages, even ones that are naturally easier for English speakers, take a lot of time and patience. There is much more to learning a language than just vocabulary words. You have to learn how the language works in order to be able to read, write, translate and converse. And learning is a gradual process. If students think they can just go to class, and that knowledge of the Cherokee language will be effortlessly transferred from teacher to student, they will be sadly disappointed. Languages take time to learn. Some, like Cherokee, will take more time, but the formula is still the same. Work patiently, steadily and thoughtfully, and you will learn.

Spanish and Russian also taught me that languages are vast systems that have a logical order to them. There are many things about languages that are predictable, even though there will be exceptions. But all the parts fit together like beautiful clockwork. When I first began studying Cherokee, I knew there was order to the language, even though I could barely catch a glimpse of it. But I had faith that it was there, and that it would come into focus over time with patience and persistence.

My belief that I would be able to learn over time has served me well. Few people realize the importance of preparing yourself mentally to study Cherokee. If you cultivate a positive outlook and have confidence in your ability to learn, you will be prepared for success. If you harbor self-doubt, you are preparing yourself for failure.

There are many attitudes that can interfere with learning Cherokee. Some students worry that their learning will always be limited, because they did not grow up hearing Cherokee spoken in their homes or communities. My own experience tells me that anyone can learn, even with little or no previous exposure to the language.

I began my studies with nothing authentically Cherokee to lean on. I didn't grow up in a Cherokee speaking family and didn't live near a Cherokee community. That doesn't mean I wasn't prepared to learn. I stood outside the language, yet everything that had happened in my life, my childhood, education, my interests in art, poetry, music, raising a family—all these experiences helped form the tools with which to learn. Most adult learners will have many tools to work with:

- Joyfulness in beginning new things, perhaps carried over from a childhood delighting in discovery

- Perseverance, developed through a desire to reach your goals, from work and family responsibilities, hurdles, disappointments, delays and successes

- Prioritizing, learned from raising children, from working, from aiming for any goal, knowing what has to come first and when, and also learned from opportunities we let pass by

- Empathy, learned from living on the earth among others, knowing that you are not just here for yourself, and wanting to reach out to others and help, and to be part of a learning community, and even to teach

- Patience, knowing that your heart's desire cannot always be reached the moment you think of it

Consider any interests you have. If you like to fish, you've learned the beauty of quiet times in nature, which will help you to listen to elders speak, to listen for clues just as you would wait quietly for a fish to bite, not disturbing the waters. You've also learned that patience will lead to success over time. If you enjoy cooking for others, that prepares you to share what you love, and to take a deep interest in people. You may also enjoy singing in a choir, or playing with other musicians. That is great preparation for working with others toward a common goal. If you enjoy reading, you've been accustomed to looking into different ways of thinking, and that prepares you to enter into the Cherokee world with an open mind. If you like mathematics, you understand the importance of organization, and will probably be watching for the bigger picture. This will help you grasp the amazing system of the Cherokee language. If you are very young, your experience will be fresh and bright, and boundless energy and optimism and that wonderful feeling of living-foreverness will carry you far. Adult learners would do well to borrow some of that optimism. You may not have grown up in a Cherokee-speaking community, but your life experience, whatever your age, is all the preparation you need.

New students should guard against being influenced by negative thinking around them, which could result in their giving up their studies. Most people have heard someone say, 'I'm just not good at languages.' Often others will nod in agreement. Maybe even some of you. It seems to be an accepted notion that some people are naturally gifted at learning languages, and some are not. This is a great excuse for someone who becomes frustrated after a few Cherokee lessons. Those students who run for the exit with 'I'm just not good at languages . . .' echoing down the hall behind them, can probably cite many instances of dogs eating their homework when they were children. I'm not sure which excuse is more believable.

I've heard students talk about other learners who are doing really well and say, 'Oh he is just a sponge for language,' or 'She has a photographic memory.' Actually, while those comments come from sincere admiration and are very kindly meant, they don't give those second-language learners credit for all the real effort and time they have put into learning Cherokee. This gets to the heart of a real misunderstanding. New students may look at the complexity of Cherokee and view anyone who seems to be making headway as possessing supernatural language ability, which in turn, makes them think they are just not up to the task. If people believe that you need a special something to learn Cherokee, like a magic ring that illuminates the mysteries of the Cherokee language, but only for the wearer, how could they even want to try? I personally have never seen such a ring. I doubt it exists.

The truth is, there is no special ring, and no special language gene that some people are born with. There is no super-power that a select few possess. If you want to learn and you apply yourself, you will succeed. Learning has nothing to do with some rare natural ability, and has everything to do with desire and commitment.

Another myth that can derail Cherokee language learners is the idea that a person can be too old to learn. Some students may think they are not up to the challenge of learning Cherokee because they feel they have trouble getting things to stick, because of what they call their *old brains*. I've heard people say that learning a language after childhood is very difficult, and becomes more difficult with every year beyond the age of eighteen.

It's true that children pick up their home language effortlessly. Why wouldn't they? Their language is woven into every aspect of their lives from the moment they are born. Very few Cherokee language learners have the opportunity to live in a truly immersive environment, surrounded by the language twenty-four hours a day for years on end. So, some might think, the situation is utterly hopeless for someone who is forty or fifty, or even—dare I say it?—over sixty. If you couple the belief that a person can be too old to learn with the idea that Cherokee is just *too* difficult, then you have a recipe for failure. 'The language is hard to begin with,' some might say, 'and I really am too old anyway.' Students who think like that often throw in the towel after learning a few words only, and leave the rest to the young learners, who they imagine to be supernaturally gifted when it comes to language learning.

I don't consider myself an amazing learner, but I am an example of someone who is very motivated and persistent. When I first took Ed's classes I didn't even know how to say Ꮢ *siyo*, 'hello.' I was in my early sixties. Not my teens, my twenties, thirties, forties or fifties—my sixties. If someone is convinced that their brain automatically turns off past a certain point, then he or she may not even try to learn Cherokee. It just isn't true. No one should let age stand in their way. I understand some students may be out of the habit of study, but study is not a bad word. It has nothing to do with merciless drilling and memorizing, necessitating the application of cold compresses to the forehead every fifteen minutes. Instead, it has everything to do with patience and a sincere desire to learn. If I can learn, others can learn.

Cherokee is not too hard. It is not too difficult. Cherokee is not blocking the road with eighteen-wheelers to keep you from making your way into the language. It is not beyond your ability to learn. It will take more time to learn Cherokee than it would to learn Spanish or French. It will take more time to find resources. It will take more time to learn vocabulary and to understand the grammar. It will take more time to learn the syllabary. But 'more time' does not equal 'more difficult.' There is nothing in Cherokee that is beyond learning. Cherokees have learned the language as children for thousands of years, and many Europeans learned the language while living among the Cherokees. It may take more time for English speakers to learn Cherokee, but only because it is so different from English. If you put one foot in front of the other in your studies, you will proceed along the path at a steady pace. If you start with the idea that the path is treacherous, you will stumble and lose heart.

Fortunately, no second-language learner need walk the path of learning alone. The Internet brings groups of Cherokee students together who support one another. Many are motivated by the desire to help the language survive. Students can share questions, answers, concerns, and helpful strategies for learning. This example of ᏍᏕ *gadugi*, the Cherokee term for 'working together cooperatively,' can be seen in action every day on social media like Facebook. Many students are finding ways to help one another. Some create Cherokee vocabulary flashcards for others to use, some share links to valuable resources, and some explain concepts that newer learners are grappling with. Others share new words they have come across, or give examples of sentences students can use in their home—the list of useful information goes on and on.

The Internet is wonderful for Cherokee students, but new learners should realize that not all information they find online is correct. Many people, with very good intentions, post about Cherokee language topics they understand imperfectly, in a sincere effort to help and to teach others. Students brand-new to Cherokee, may see these online posts or 'lessons' and assume that they are correct, and pass them along to others who are also new to learning. Misinformation travels like wildfire on the Internet. Every student needs to look carefully at what they find online, and ask a trusted source for help if they are not sure. Fortunately, many Cherokee language groups online have a number of advanced Cherokee learners, and sometimes native speakers, who will be very happy to verify information and clear up any confusion.

Motivation for learning Cherokee varies from person to person. Some want to learn because they are tribal members or have Cherokee ancestry. Many want to be able to carry on simple conversations with others, or to be able to teach their children or grandchildren. Some have the goal of being able to read old documents such as the *Cherokee Phoenix* or the New Testament translated into Cherokee. It is truly magical to read a passage that was written in 1833 when the Cherokee syllabary was new—like walking back in time and looking over the shoulders of some of the first Cherokees to write in syllabary, just as they put ink on paper. There are countless treasures that a knowledge of Cherokee can help to unlock, and the language is interwoven with all aspects of Cherokee life and culture.

There are others who come to the language, not because of a direct connection to Cherokee, but because of an interest in the language itself, or an interest in linguistics. They may be interested in comparing Cherokee to other languages they have learned. Still others may be drawn to learn because of their study of the history of the Cherokee people.

The reasons for beginning a study of Cherokee may be varied. However, almost all learners come together in their desire to contribute to the preservation of the language in some way.

◆   ◆   ◆

The Cherokee language is in trouble. According to UNESCO (United Nations Educational, Scientific and Cultural Organization), Oklahoma Cherokee, spoken among the Cherokee Nation and the United Keetoowah Band, is considered definitely endangered. That means that children are no longer learning Cherokee as their first language growing up. Cherokee spoken in North Carolina among the Eastern Band of Cherokees is considered to be severely endangered, meaning it is only spoken by the grandparent or older generations, and while parent generations may understand the language, they no longer speak Cherokee among themselves or to their children. [1]

This situation is dire. Cherokee is no longer being learned in the home by children, and the elders will be gone within a generation or two. There is an old saying: 'When an old person dies, a library burns down.' A lifetime of experience and knowledge, of memories and dreams dies along with that person. Many people have had the experience of losing a loved one, and even many years later thinking of things they wished they had asked them. It is a truly helpless feeling, knowing that you missed an opportunity that can never return. Now, imagine what it means if an entire language dies. Libraries beyond counting would burn to the ground, and along with them, irreplaceable information.

In order to imagine what a world without native speakers would be like, it's necessary to appreciate what the world is like with Cherokee speakers. Every individual in a community has his or her own experiences and stores of knowledge. One person may know the names of some plants and their medicinal uses, another person may know others. Some people will know one way of telling a traditional story, but others may have heard different versions. Their knowledge and traditions have been passed down to them through generations.

Those who have taken Ed Fields' class have seen glimpses of an older Cherokee world. They've heard Ed describe a fuller way of speaking, a way that few use today. They may have been in class when Ed spoke of a word he hadn't heard since he was young, a word not in any dictionary. They've heard about elders long ago predicting things that have since come to pass. They've heard Ed talk about plants. About strange happenings. About knowing things. When Ed teaches, he lets his students catch a glimpse of slender threads still connected to an older way of life. A way of life that is on the point of vanishing. When those slender threads are gone, only the memory of what has been shared will remain.

If you are thinking of learning Cherokee, make every effort to learn what you can from a speaker. If they speak to you, listen. If they teach you, learn. What they have to share is priceless.

Words may even hold clues to forgotten cultural practices. I was very surprised to find that the Cherokee name for my state of Florida, DCᏝM&ᏠᏯT ᏉSSᎩ *ahliyoluhvsgii sgadugi*, had a different meaning than what I thought. DCᏝM&ᏠᏯT *ahliyoluhvsgii* means, 'it floats,' whereas ᏉSSᎩ *sgadugi* is a way of saying, 'state.' I had previously thought it was a recently added, humorous name. Florida. A floating state. Haha. But I was wrong. Very wrong.

In her book *The Cherokee Syllabary: Writing the People's Perseverance*, author Ellen Cushman recounts that, in discussions with a fluent speaker, she learned that DCᏝM&ᏠᏯT ᏉSSᎩ *ahliyoluhvsgii sgadugi* is what he had heard in his family as the name for Florida, and that it referred to a time when Cherokees would go down to Florida to harvest wild rice, which floats.[2] Far from being a humorous name, it actually carries important cultural and historical information about the Cherokee people. Imagine how much information like this has already been lost, and how much would be beyond retrieval if the language were to disappear.

The precarious state of the Cherokee language lends poignancy to every effort to learn. It is heartbreaking to think the language could be on the brink of extinction. If the language survives, it will be a different language than that which is currently spoken by the last generation of native speakers. Children are not growing up in an immersed environment, where parents and grandparents surround them with Cherokee. A great deal of vocabulary has already been lost.

There are those who believe that, in the future, there could be a community of second-language learners who bring the language into their own homes and teach their children, and that new speakers will be born into the language. In the meantime, the language will be in the hands of second-language learners entirely. That is a hard pill to swallow. In perhaps only one or two generations, there will be no born-in-the-language speakers to turn to for clarification, for answers, for help with the language. There will be no speakers to unravel difficult passages in old documents, to gently lead others inside the language, to help others think in Cherokee.

Considering how grim the situation looks for Cherokee, students may wonder if anything they do could ever be more than a drop in the bucket. And how can learning a language help it to survive, if there will be no more first language speakers in a generation or two?

The answer is that every little drop in the bucket can help. A student doesn't have to be dedicated to becoming fluent in order to make a mark. Even casually learning some basic greetings and conversation can have an impact. Perhaps those words will be shared with family members. Even if they show little interest now, it's possible that they will remember their exposure to the language later, and feel the desire to learn. If you use only a few words in your community, perhaps at a store where you shop, you might awaken an interest in Cherokee in someone with whom you spoke, or with someone who only overheard. Awakening an interest in the language is of great value. You never know what a single spoken word in Cherokee might lead to. There may be others you come into contact with who may become interested in studying grammar or linguistics. A number of years down the line, they may publish papers which help preserve valuable information about the structure or history of the Cherokee language.

If students are very motivated and learn a great deal, they may be able to teach Cherokee in their communities, and reach a large number of people. Some of their students may go on to share the language and teach it to their children and grandchildren. Some students will learn to translate, and will join community efforts to decipher and analyze old documents.

There is no level of Cherokee learning which is too small to matter. If you have the drive to learn a lot and limitless time, you are in the wonderful position of being able to aim for the stars. But if you are busy with work and family and have less time, it is still worth learning what you can. And, on a personal level, you will have the satisfaction of knowing that the same words you speak were spoken by Sequoyah and other Cherokees long ago.

Once a student decides to take the plunge into Cherokee language studies, there are still situations that come up which can make it hard to have time for language learning. Families and jobs must always come first. Every Cherokee student has to put their studies on the back burner at one time or another. I have done it, and you will too. But there is no timetable to which students must adhere. Learning Cherokee is not a race. We all work at it when we can, knowing we can resume our study when time opens up again. There is no need to feel that being sidetracked or delayed will take away from your ability to learn when you do have time.

Whatever your reason for learning Cherokee and however much time you have to devote to study, keep a positive outlook and know that you can accomplish your goals. Learning Cherokee may take longer than learning some other languages, but it is still within your grasp, and your time will be richly repaid. Little by little, you will be learning to think in Cherokee and to understand the Cherokee worldview which will, in turn, enrich your own way of looking at the world. Remember that learning Cherokee is not an activity that can be completed and checked off in X amount of time, but rather, a wonderful lifelong journey.

The Cherokee language needs our help. Let's all work together, ᎦᏚᎩ *gadugi*, and see what we can accomplish. We all have the power to shape the future with our deliberate actions today.

CHAPTER THREE

Where To Start?

ED FIELDS

ᏏᏲ Ꮩ ᎬᎥ *siyo ale wado*, 'Hello, and thank you' for staying with me for this chapter. I hope it helps you. But I must tell you that I don't know all the classes and programs and ways out there to learn Cherokee. And new ones may be out there by the time you read this. But I will list some.

I guess one way to start is to figure out where you want to learn. Do you want to learn at home, at university or elsewhere? Do you want free or to pay for it or a combination? Of course, even those who are paying for an education can use the free ones too. I'm not saying there is only one way. And free does not mean inferior—it can offer smaller class sizes so the teacher can spend more time with you. And your fellow students may already have some or a lot of Cherokee language knowledge or culture that they share with you too. Sometimes older people who have lived in the language and culture will not attend a university class but will come to a free class in the community or online. And sometimes it can be more fun because there's less stress, less pressure of passing exams and of worrying about grade-point averages and of worrying about graduating from freshman to sophomore and so on. Instead you can relax and learn more at your own pace.

One way to learn Cherokee is to find a relative or friend who is a fluent first-language Cherokee speaker or one who knows a lot of Cherokee and learn from them. Some of you may be thinking 'I have someone like that but they never try to teach me' or 'if they want me to learn, why don't they volunteer to teach me?' The answer, and remember everyone is different even your elders, is because elders who grew up in the culture usually wait for you to come to them.

You come to them and tell them that you want to be taught and ask them to teach you. Remember, not all elders are like this but yours may be. So if you have a relative or friend who is a Cherokee speaker and you want to learn from them, ask them to teach you. If they say they don't know how to teach, then ask them to 'just share' what they can. Or if they say they don't know enough Cherokee to teach you, then ask them to just teach you what they know.

Now, if an elder does volunteer (sometimes they might because not all elders are the same, just like you are different too), but if they volunteer to teach you or to share or to help you learn and you don't accept their offer, then don't expect them to keep volunteering or offering again and again. If you ask and they agree to teach you, or they volunteer and you accept, then carry through on your part of it. Because words are one thing and actions are another and it takes both. That is, if you say you want to learn Cherokee but then only do it once or twice or a handful of times and then begin to stray off into doing other things or not come any more or not pay attention and such, then don't blame the elder for realizing that you were not really sincere. And don't blame them for doing something else with their time and energy. Maybe someone else wants to learn and the elder has instead focused on you because you're related or you're a friend or you asked first or such, but now as they say 'all deals are off' and the elder is free to teach someone who is sincere or the elder is free to do something else with their time and energy. One only has so much time and energy, use it wisely.

Another way to learn Cherokee is at a university. I've had some people tell me that they looked at what some universities offered and the cost of it and could not afford it and so they were glad for the free classes that the Cherokee Nation offered. I've also had some people want to know if some university or some professor was good. But I do not know all the universities and professors, and it is best that you research. It also depends on what you want to learn and how much you want to learn.

I wish every one of you could have a Cherokee language teacher who is fluent and knows the Cherokee worldview and is able to help you learn Cherokee, how to think in Cherokee, how to be able to figure out Cherokee words and sentences for yourself, why a word means what it does, why a word or sentence is done in a certain way and other things. So that when your time with the teacher is ended and you're on your own, you'll be able to think in Cherokee, to figure things out for yourself as much as possible, because someday the teacher will no longer be there and you'll be on your own. So I wish all of you could have a teacher who teaches you how to stand on your own two feet in the language and walk into the future in the language.

This is especially important when you want to translate. Translating takes a lot of knowledge and thought and figuring things out because Cherokee and English are not an exact fit. And this is also important when your job or work requires that you come up with new Cherokee words for modern things that our elders did not have back then so did not name back then.

You and future learners will carry on the Cherokee language and the Cherokee worldview. You want to hold to both tightly. We can't be lax about it, we can't be too busy or too rushed or too anything that makes us want to just say 'well, this is the word in English and this is the word in Cherokee so we'll just use this Cherokee word as it basically means the same,' only to not have the real Cherokee meaning and the real Cherokee worldview behind that word or phrase.

Instead, when coming up with a name for a modern thing you want the word or phrase to be a Cherokee word or phrase that is grounded in the Cherokee language and the Cherokee worldview. So that the real Cherokee meaning is there.

Of course, those of you who are not going to try to get a job in the language or to work in it or do not want to learn to be fluent or have the Cherokee worldview, that is also up to you. But there are a lot of fun and interesting things to learning the Cherokee language, and you might find yourself having adventures in the Cherokee language every day. On the other hand, if learning the sounds and some words is all you can get for whatever reason or all you can afford or is all you want, then every little bit helps save the Cherokee language.

And keep in mind that even in a good university course you'll still have to constantly research to make sure you're getting the real Cherokee word, real Cherokee sentence and real Cherokee meaning, because teachers and their helpers are human, they make mistakes, make typos, have an 'off day' and word-processing programs sometimes auto-correct words they ought not correct and things can get overlooked and so on. So always research.

Another way to learn Cherokee, would be hiring someone who is good in Cherokee to tutor or teach you Cherokee in person or online. Ask around before hiring though. Remember sometimes free offers a lot.

Also, if you're not the one hiring but know of someone who is hiring a tutor or who has hired a tutor then you can ask the one doing the learning from the tutor to teach you what they're learning. Or get a group together so the one being taught can share with everyone in the group. But do this respectfully. If the tutor or teacher teaches you something and says to not tell others then respect that. It may be something personal to that tutor or teacher or something sacred that they only want shared with you.

Another way to learn Cherokee in person or by online is to attend a Cherokee language class from a recognized Cherokee Community

Organization. You can search the websites of the three federally recognized tribal governments or contact them and ask for information. Maybe they have a Cherokee Community Organization near you. But if you find that you don't have one near you, then maybe they'll have classes you can attend over the Internet. If you don't have Internet, I've had students use free Internet from a library or eatery or other place to attend class. It's not ideal for them, but they somehow manage it because they want to do whatever it takes to attend class and learn Cherokee. It's that important to them.

Or maybe the Cherokee Community Organization can pair you up with a member of their community who knows more than you and is willing to teach you. Or maybe you two—or more—could help each other learn. Or the Cherokee Community Organization may post classes they've done on their Internet website and you can watch and listen to the classes and learn like that.

The three federally recognized tribes and Community Organizations may also have free downloadable Cherokee language learning materials. For instance, Cherokee Nation has free fonts, keyboard, posters, and more.

Another way to learn Cherokee is to take a class offered by one of the three federally recognized Cherokee tribal governments. You can search their websites or contact their language departments or help/information centers and ask what they offer.

Some of these classes or programs may be for adults only, but others may be for both adults and children. For instance, in the Cherokee Nation Online Cherokee Language Classes the majority of learners are adults, but a few parents attend with their children. And, occasionally, they attend with their babies. That way their babies can hear the language as young as possible and maybe learn the language as they grow, or at least have their language-'ears' (brains) attuned early so the Cherokee language is familiar to them. Because you are never too old or too young to learn Cherokee.

For those of you who can't attend any of the above, keep in mind that if you know someone who is attending any of the above that

39

you can always ask them to share with you what they're learning. And with technology these days you don't even have to be in the same town or state or nation as them.

Same if you're a parent of a child and that child is going to a Cherokee class in their school or in an after-school program or in their community, when they come home have your child teach you what they learned that day. If other family members or friends want to learn, you could do a Cherokee language learning group in your home or community. Having your child teach you also encourages your child. And it helps your child learn. Because teaching the language tends to make the one doing the teaching concentrate and learn and figure out a host of other things about the Cherokee language in order to be able to teach it. Teaching Cherokee is a good way to learn, providing the one learning-and-teaching is going about it in a good way, a diligent way, a worthy way.

Another way to learn the Cherokee language is in a Cherokee church. In the past there were many of these. But these days you'll have to look around to find a Cherokee church that still teaches how to read from the Cherokee Bible, still sings in Cherokee, and still preaches in the Cherokee language. In past days, some Cherokee preachers would preach in the Cherokee language then repeat it in the English language. You had a Cherokee-English translating service going on that you could learn from. Cherokee churches that still do these things are getting rare, even almost extinct, as most use the English language nowadays. ᎤᏁᏝᏄᎥᎯ *Unetlanvhi*, 'Creator, God' created the Cherokee language and gave it to bless us, to enrich us and the world. Maybe Cherokee-teaching churches will make a comeback when more people want to learn the Cherokee language for free at church.

Another way to learn Cherokee, perhaps because you have no other way or because you choose to do it this way, is on your own. With technology these days you can do many things online, but be prepared to spend time searching online for Cherokee language websites, videos in Cherokee, audios in Cherokee, and free Cherokee language materials at tribal government websites that you can access or download. And be prepared to spend time searching for free online Cherokee dictionaries, newspapers, other Cherokee texts, audio, video resources online or at public digital libraries and university digital libraries or online archive sites. Be prepared to search for hard-copy resources at public libraries, university libraries, inter-library loan programs and paying for copies of things you may need. Some resources are free or online, others you'll have to be prepared to buy as you gather those Cherokee language resources you need to build your own Cherokee home library. And be prepared to do everything you can think of to surround yourself with the sight and sound of the Cherokee language every day and as often as possible. You'll need to be extra vigilant and constantly research to make sure you're getting real Cherokee words with real Cherokee meanings and real Cherokee resources.

And, of course, another way to learn is to do a combination of two or more of the above ways. Always being vigilant and constantly researching.

But this is true too of all of these ways—you will need to constantly research to make sure you're getting the real Cherokee words and real Cherokee meanings because people are human and sometimes make mistakes. This is why it is good to have the old writings to be able to go back to—the Cherokee Bible, the Cherokee newspapers, and other old Cherokee translated works—and check them for our elders' words and meanings and such. Creating your own Cherokee home library that you can have handy at any time is a good thing.

You need to surround yourself with the sight and sound of the Cherokee language every day, as often as possible. For instance, gather Cherokee materials to create your own audio and video library of Cherokee and watch and/or listen to Cherokee each day or at least as often as you can. Put sticky notes on items all over your home, with each item's name written in Cherokee phonetics (or syllabary first if you want) so that every time you see it you're reminded to say it, then say it out loud and over time you'll associate the Cherokee word with that item. When you get to where you can think of that item in Cherokee without the sticky note reminder then add to that sticky note the item's name in syllabary (or simply switch the sticky note of the phonetic name with a sticky note of the syllabary name).

Hearing and seeing Cherokee every day is good and helps. But using Cherokee is even better. So find ways to use Cherokee in your everyday life. For instance, if you enjoy writing, write in Cherokee. At first you might not know enough Cherokee, maybe you only know a few words, but as time goes by make it a point to learn more words that you can write. Write grocery lists, to-do lists, reminders. Write journal entries, diary entries, letters. Write poems. Write short stories or novels. Write articles, family history, books. Write comic strips and mangas. Write scripts and plays. If you write, just think of ways to use Cherokee in your writing life.

If you paint or draw, while painting or drawing think in Cherokee and say out loud in Cherokee each thing you're painting or drawing. Each item on the face, think it and say it out loud in Cherokee when you paint or draw it. Each thing in a landscape, in a room, and so on. You can draw, ink or color comics and think Cherokee and even write Cherokee speech bubbles and such. Or paint pictures and find ways to put Cherokee words, phrases, sentences in your painting. Just let Cherokee and your creativity merge and flow together.

If you like to sing, you can sing in Cherokee. You can find the old hymn books free on the Internet. Dennis Sixkiller's radio program—*Cherokee Voices, Cherokee Sounds*—has a lot of Cherokee singing, and you can sing along. And you can also make up your own Cherokee songs. If you don't have enough Cherokee yet, you can take the Cherokee Psalms or verses from the Bible and turn them into songs. Or turn words from the Cherokee newspaper or other Cherokee resources into a song. Or you can sing what words you do know and add to them as you go along. If you only know a few words at first just start with those, singing them over and over to a melody, and then make it a point to find other words to add to your song.

Like to play sports or woodwork or cook or sew or garden? Whatever you like to do, begin letting it and Cherokee merge and flow together. You will learn Cherokee faster.

Talk to yourself—they used to say this was a bad thing but nowadays they say it's a sign of genius. They say, Einstein and other geniuses spoke to themselves. So be a genius and talk to yourself in Cherokee. And talk to your dog, cat, horse or other animal. They'll also even learn Cherokee too. Of course, some people talk to their car, their TV, their computer or other things, so why not talk in Cherokee? (See Figure 3.1).

Figure 3.1. Boy Talking to Dog

Have a daily 'Cherokee-only' session where you make a choice each day to use Cherokee instead of English, and then do it. Maybe the first week, talk only in Cherokee for 30 seconds daily. Then the next week, go to a full minute. And the next week, for two minutes. Just increase each week . . . to five, eight, ten and so on until you get to where you can do an amount that is longer and that you're pleased with. If 30 seconds is too long or too short a time for you to begin with, then start at a length of time that fits your needs. Also, you can make your own Cherokee Language Phrase Book of Cherokee words, phrases, sentences and conversations. Then use it when necessary. And make it a point to add more words, phrases and sentences to it as the days, weeks and months go by.

You can make your own pictorial Cherokee dictionary. Cut out pictures from magazines or draw them or print them out, then label them in Cherokee syllabary and/or phonetics. You can stop there if you wish, as this will help your brain begin to match the picture with the Cherokee syllabary and/or phonetics for the picture. Or you can add a definition in English, but know that the English words may hinder your brain from associating the picture with the Cherokee syllabary and/or phonetics as quickly or as well as using only the picture and the syllabary and/or phonetics.

You can make up and play your own Cherokee language games. For instance, the Cherokee language movie game: when you're going to watch a movie or video of some sort, pick out five or so words in Cherokee that you'll say out loud whenever you see the image of them on the screen. Say you're going to watch a family movie so you pick out the Cherokee words DᎣᏒSB *asgayv*, DᏂᎥB *age/h/yv*, DᎫᏟ *atsutsa*, DᏂᎬᏟ *age/h/yutsa*, ᏩᎤ *wesa*, (man, woman, boy, girl, cat) or you're going to watch a nature documentary and you pick out the Cherokee words TᏉE *itlugv*, DᏂᏇᎣᏟᎩ *atsilvsgi*, DSᎣᏒS *agasga*, TS *iga*, OᏒRT *usvi*, ZᏪb *noqu/i/si*, (tree, flower, rain, day, night, star) then every time one of those images comes on your screen you say the Cherokee word for that image. As your Cherokee vocabulary grows you'll be able to say more words and make the game more challenging and learning for yourself. And you can have family and friends play the game along with you.

Just remember to have fun playing it and to keep it fun, don't get frustrated or so exact you tie yourself in knots—or everyone else up in knots.

When doing some action, say what you're doing in Cherokee, ᎦᎵᏍᏓᏴᎲᏍᎦ *galisdayvhvsga*, 'I'm eating,' ᏥᏰᏫᏍᎦ *tsiyewisga*, 'I'm sewing,' ᏥᎯᎵ *tsihili*, 'I'm driving,' and so on. Then as your vocabulary grows add to that ᎠᏂ ᏥᎩᎠ *a'ni tsigia*, 'I'm eating a strawberry,' ᎠᎿᏬ ᏥᏰᏫᏍᎦ *ahnawo tsiyewisga*, 'I'm sewing a shirt,' ᎥᏓᎵ ᎢᏗᏢ ᏫᏥᎯᎵ *vdali iditlv witsihili*, 'I'm driving to the lake.' You can even add on to that by saying what color or amount or size or why you're doing what you're doing and so on.

Just think of ways that you can see and hear Cherokee every day. Think of ways to surround yourself with the Cherokee language. And then create that learning environment.

Also, change the way you think about learning. Instead of saying 'I have to study Cherokee' or 'I must learn Cherokee verbs today'—which has a heavy, tiring feel to it and puts a burden type feel on your mind and heart and even body—say 'I get to study Cherokee' or 'I get to learn Cherokee verbs today' which has a light, energetic feel to it and puts a joyful type feel on your mind and heart and body.

Find a place that is teaching Cherokee or a place where people work in Cherokee and volunteer to help in some way. That way you'll hear Cherokee and get to ask questions.

Have you ever had a TV or radio jingle or a song lyric play over and over in your mind? You can use that to help yourself. When you come across Cherokee words, phrases or sentences that seem to be taking a little longer to learn, turn them into a jingle or song. It doesn't matter how good or bad you sing, that's not what it's about, it's about you learning Cherokee. If you don't have a jingle or song melody of your own to use, then use one from past TV or radio ads or childhood songs or other source and put Cherokee with it. If you want, you can even try to sing like the singer of the jingle or song does, even do their hand movements and such—or even dance. Learning Cherokee doesn't have to be a stiff, boring experience. It can be as fun as you can make it.

But now, let's be serious for a moment. Because I have to caution you. Because I've had people ask me 'how long does it take to learn Cherokee?' or 'what are the levels that I can track that let me know I'm learning?' or some other type of question about ways to determine how far they've come and how far they have to go.

Levels and stages and measuring units are hard to determine. For one thing, each of you learns differently. I wish that all of you could have a Cherokee Language course that is tailor-made to you in every way. Another reason it's hard to determine levels, stages and measuring units is because learning institutions or organizations have different ways to measure.

Units of measurements give you a guide, show you where you're at and how far you have to go, and knowing how far you've come and how far you've left to go may encourage or inspire you, but it may also discourage and uninspire you. You need to know yourself. Know whether knowing how far you've come and how far you've left to go will encourage or discourage you. Then take the steps needed. If knowing how far you've come and how far you've left to go encourages you, then look up some measurements used and see where you are on that 'map' and where you need to go and then head in that direction. If knowing how far you've come and how far you've left to go discourages you, then ignore levels, stages and measuring units and just carry on learning, you'll eventually get where you're going anyway.

Those of you taking the Online Cherokee Language Classes, if you're expecting that a few class hours each week for ten weeks will be enough to learn Cherokee, then know that, yes, you will learn some Cherokee, but in order to learn a lot or to be fluent in Cherokee you'll need to do outside classroom learning time too. Because there is not enough inside classroom time, between answering questions and sharing culture and such the classroom time goes by fast. And some classes have a lot of students with each asking a few questions, or a few students with each asking a lot of questions.

Classroom time can help you learn, and when you run into questions with your outside classroom learning time, if there's enough classroom time left after the lesson, then you may get to ask some of the questions in class. And when you do become fluent, the online class can help you continue your listening and comprehension skills, retain what you've learned and give you a way you can help others learn Cherokee in the chat room.

Learning also depends on your goal. How much of the Cherokee language do you want to learn? To reach 'a lot' or 'fluent'—and especially 'fluent'—you'll have to study outside the classroom as well as in the classroom. To be fluent, you'll need to learn how to think, reason and respond to your everyday life in Cherokee so that when no Cherokee speaker is around, no Cherokee teacher, no Cherokee instructor then you'll still be able to have the Cherokee worldview and be able to walk in the Cherokee language during your daily life and activities.

Many students are trying to learn, and even to be fluent, and they attend classes at or from various places and listen to teachers, but to be fluent it takes more than listening. In class you need to set yourself to learning and digesting what the teacher is teaching. If you don't understand, ask questions. Make sure you not only know, but understand. Because if you're not able to do any thinking on your own in Cherokee, but only parrot the teacher, then what happens when you don't have the teacher anymore?

And, teacher, are they really learning Cherokee if they cannot walk in their daily lives in it? Someday the teacher will be taken from the equation. When that happens will all the Cherokee language that the student "learned" disappear like a vapor that drifts and fades and no longer holds a form? If asked what an item or object is in Cherokee and why it's called that or even what something should be named and why—can the student tell you?

Students, if you want to learn a tiny amount to maybe a medium amount of Cherokee, you can spend some time in the classroom and do that or even teach yourself by gathering written materials, audio materials, video materials and studying them until you learn. But to learn a lot or learn to be fluent in the language it takes more than just classroom attendance—even more than being active in class—because you'll also have to study outside of the classroom.

A good teacher in classroom time can help you learn how to think for yourself in Cherokee, how to think in the Cherokee worldview, and help you learn not only what something is in Cherokee but why it is. But you have to help yourself learn too.

You need to learn how to help yourself because first-language Cherokee teachers are scarce now and getting more so. The day may come when the next Cherokee teachers out there will be those who have learned Cherokee as a second-language and not as their first-language. If not done vigilantly, this can allow some first language loss of words, meanings, worldview. So teacher and student need to be vigilant that what is being taught are real Cherokee words, meanings, worldview and what is being learned are real Cherokee words, meanings, worldview.

If false or fake words, meanings, worldview get taught and learned instead of the real and true, then the Cherokee language and worldview changes and loses more and more over time until it is really more endangered than before. More endangered because now the fake and false have taken over and replaced the real and true.

False or fake Cherokee words, meanings, and worldview harm real and true ones. False or fake ones do not help the Cherokee language be saved, do not help it grow or thrive. False or fake ones aid in destroying the Cherokee language. It aids in making it more endangered than before because the fake and false get taught and accepted and passed on to others, while the real and true get lost or rejected and not passed on to others. Don't let the Cherokee language become more endangered than before. Help the Cherokee language live. Help the Cherokee language grow and thrive.

If you're feeling a little discouraged, just remember that if you start and don't stop, you'll learn. How fast, how much and how well you learn will depend on what you do after you start.

When learning the Cherokee language you have choices concerning the amount you want to learn. Those of you who want to be fluent are really seeking to learn a worldview, that is, how to look at the world and the things in it from a Cherokee mindset and to think, reason, figure things out in that Cherokee mindset, from that Cherokee worldview. You want to be able to carry on a real conversation in Cherokee, which requires processing what you hear so that you can reply in a way that makes sense, that is, you will be able to communicate with other Cherokee speakers, even elders who are first-language speakers.

The language is endangered and needs help. And knowing even a little Cherokee and sharing that is better than not knowing any and not sharing any. So if you only learn the sounds and pass those on someone can take those and add more learning to them, or if you only learn some words and pass those on, that's better than not knowing anything and not passing anything on. Every little bit helps and you can be a helper to saving the language.

And those of you who are seeking to be fluent, take heart. Patrick Del Percio and Mary Rae have proven it's possible to reach the fluent level. But they had to make choices and you will too. They chose to learn in a classroom plus learn outside the classroom on their own—they each set themselves to studying at home; creating a Cherokee home library by gathering Cherokee materials and resources they could study, gathering and listening to audio and video of Cherokee, creating their own immersion times in the Cherokee language, seeking others to help them when possible and helping others learn Cherokee by sharing and teaching the Cherokee they had learned. Because when you share and teach, not only are others helped, but you—the one doing the sharing and teaching—are helped too.

There are other things you can do to learn Cherokee. Just think of ways to help yourself learn. To surround yourself in Cherokee.

To create your own time, every day if possible, of immersion in the Cherokee language. Even if you're taking a class, continue to study and learn outside of classroom time. (See Figure 3.2)

Someday class will end, teacher will be gone, you'll be on your own. What then of the Cherokee you had learned? Will it fade in time, be a fond memory—or will you have equipped yourself to continue onward in your Cherokee journey, doing what you can to learn and continuing to seek ways to proceed onward in Cherokee?

I still enjoy learning the Cherokee language. Like with any language that is to live and thrive, it must grow and the vocabulary grows too. So I will continue to learn new Cherokee words that get added to the Cherokee language all my life long. And I will continue to learn old Cherokee words that have been overlooked in the old writings. I still enjoy looking up the old words and reading the old writings. And I still enjoy figuring out words for things the Cherokee people and elders did not have back then but we have today. I enjoy looking at the world through Cherokee heart, eyes and mind that the Cherokees back then helped teach me and still teach me today through their written works and audio works.

Figure 3.2. Girl Studying

Learning Cherokee is fun and satisfying. Wherever you are in your Cherokee journey and whatever level you're on, I hope you'll create your own Cherokee learning environment and learn some Cherokee every day. You'll eventually get to where you're going. I wish for you all to get to where you're going.

ᏯᏆᏚᎳ ᎢᏨᏚᎵᎥ ᎤᎵᎻᏃᏍᏗᏱ *yaquadula itsadulihv witsiluhisdiyi*, 'I would like for you all to reach your destination.'

CHAPTER FOUR

If I Can Learn, So Can You

MARY RAE

It would be nice if I could say I've arrived at a state of Cherokee-all-knowingness. But that isn't true. Not by any means. But I am further along the path than some, and would like to help others and share my thoughts on how to begin learning, how to approach problems and find information, and how to understand deeply. These are not things that I just knew. I've done quite a lot of stumbling, backtracking and reassessment along the way, and am sure to do more in the future. I wasn't born knowing how to learn Cherokee. But I have been persistent, and that is key. I learned from Ed Fields that when I stumble, I should get up and try again. When I am confused, I should stay calm and research until I find my bearings. Anyone learning Cherokee can do the same. The Cherokee language is open to all who want to learn and who want to help the language survive.

Studying Cherokee can be a wonderful adventure, but some people are practically allergic to the word 'study.' They might have had unpleasant experiences in school, and might associate studying with isolation, grueling rote memorization and boredom. For anyone who sees the word 'study' and instantly pictures a student secured to a desk by heavy chains, while all their friends run free in the grass just outside their window, I would like to suggest that studying Cherokee can actually be fun. Yes, fun.

Think about what studying means. When you study you are giving very close attention to your subject. As tedious as this may sound at first, the desire to study something can arise out of joyfulness. When I was a little girl, my sister and I collected leaves from different trees in the woods. We would take them home and carefully iron them between two sheets of wax paper, then label them. If we weren't sure which trees they belonged to, we would look them up in a book, or ask our parents or older siblings. I remember holding the leaves up to the light, turning them from front to back to study the different veining patterns. Sometimes we drew them. It was magical.

There was nothing tedious or boring about leaves in our minds. We were so excited to learn more, and waited patiently for the next season when we could begin collecting again. Small bright-green leaves in the spring, large dark green leaves in the summer, brilliant yellow, red and orange leaves in the fall, and only a few brown winter leaves along with evergreen needles. We would iron them carefully between two sheets of wax paper and label them. When we were done, we would slide the sheets into a drawer for safe-keeping. We wanted to know what the leaves looked like in all four seasons, and nothing could speed the year along, but we were in no hurry. Why did we go to all that trouble? Because we wanted to learn. To us, it wasn't work at all. We spent our happiest hours in the woods, and the desire to learn about leaves grew out of that happiness.

If you approach Cherokee in the same way, with a sense of wonder, and you study it carefully, it will never become drudgery. Let it be a natural outgrowth of your desire to learn. When you begin to see how different Cherokee is from English, and how complex the verbs are, don't shy away. Instead, think of Cherokee as a beautiful mystery that you are entering into. You will look around carefully, see the language from different perspectives, and begin to make sense of it, little by little. Keep that sense of awe in your heart and you will learn.

Most students are in a hurry to learn Cherokee. While there is a real urgency to save the Cherokee language, the goal is for people to care, to take an interest in the language, and to begin learning. Once a student is committed to the language, there is no rush. At some point early on in their studies, Cherokee students may realize how much there is to learn, and decide to launch into their learning at lightning speed. It's understandable. I certainly felt like that when I was beginning. It seems simple: Learn as much as possible as quickly as possible, and you'll be on your way to saving the language.

It is tempting to think that you can master the language in record time, if only you apply enough effort, but that strategy will backfire. Cherokee can't be learned in depth by cramming. If you try, you will miss important concepts along the way. Later, you will have no choice but to go back and re-learn, or, better said, actually learn.

It helps to think small and start with one thing at a time. Learning a few things very well lays the groundwork for progress. Patience is essential. Mastery of a few limited topics is much better than a slight and imperfect knowledge of many. There is great satisfaction in knowing something well, no matter how elementary. Simple vocabulary such as numbers can be the building blocks upon which phrases are built. That may sound too simple to some. Numbers? Child's play. Many beginning students can easily rattle off the numbers one to ten in Cherokee. But there is more to learning than that.

It's important to realize that recognizing and repeating a word you see is not the same as really knowing it. Knowing a word would involve being able to call it up from memory and to use it freely. If you use Cherokee numbers to tell time, for example, you will be incorporating the language into your everyday life.

One might wonder why numbers are a good place to start.

Surely learning about verbs and phrases is more pressing, some might think. There is really no wrong way to start, but mastering numbers early on gives beginners the opportunity to quickly begin thinking in Cherokee. Using numbers to tell time, for example, has immediate application in your own life.

Think how many times a day we look at the time on our phones, our laptops or our watches. Your morning might begin like this: 'Seven thirty-two—I still have time to get some coffee.' In the afternoon one glance at you phone reminds you: 'Three twenty-seven—Almost time to pick up the kids.' Your hectic evening might get the best of you: 'Twelve minutes after six?—Forgot to set the timer. Burned the brownies. Again.' The last example comes directly from my own experience. But the truth is, most of us have busy lives, and we are constantly checking the time.

If we replaced even one-fourth of those time-checks with telling time in Cherokee, we would be learning numbers in a very meaningful way, since knowing the time is vital to all we do. Telling time is a very easy way to begin learning numbers and to bring your Cherokee vocabulary home and into everyday use. Right now I'm looking at my clock and thinking, ᏓᎳᏚ ᎢᏯᏔᏬᏍᏔᏅ ᎤᏓᎷᎳ ᏦᎢ *daladu iyatawostanv udalula tsoi*, 'sixteen minutes before three.' Think of how many times you've checked the time already today. You could have used those opportunities to think and speak in Cherokee.

Telling time is really quite simple. In Cherokee, you count from one to twenty-nine minutes after the hour, and from twenty-nine minutes to one minute before the hour. ᏓᎳᏚ ᎢᏯᏔᏬᏍᏔᏅ ᎤᏓᎷᎳ ᏦᎢ *daladu iyatawostanv udalula tsoi*— 'sixteen minutes before three.' ᏓᎳᏚ ᎢᏯᏔᏬᏍᏔᏅ ᎤᎶᏒᏍᏗ ᏦᎢ *daladu iyatawostanv ulosvsdi tsoi*— 'sixteen minutes *after* three.' The half-hour is expressed as ᎠᏰᏟ *ayehli*, 'half' or 'middle.' For example, ᏦᎢ ᎠᏰᏟ *tsoi ayehli* would be 'three-thirty.' It should be encouraging to know that you only have to know numbers one through twenty-nine in order to tell time in Cherokee. If you don't already know the numbers you can easily find how to write and say the numbers in any Cherokee dictionary or course book.

Aside from knowing numbers one to twenty-nine, you will need this basic vocabulary to talk about the time:

ᎠᏩ ᎠᏓᎢᎵ *hila ahli'ili*, 'What time is it?'

ᎠᏓᎢᎵᏒ *ahli'ilisv*, 'The time is . . .'

ᎢᏯᏩᏌᏍᏓᏅᎥ *iyatawostanv* or ᎢᏴᏩᏌᏍᏓᏅᎥ *iyutawostanv*, 'minutes'

ᎤᏓᎳ *udalula*, 'until' or 'before'

ᎤᎶᏏᏍᏗ *ulosvsdi*, 'past' or 'after'

ᎠᏰᎵ *ayehli*, 'half' or 'half past' or 'middle'

Start by writing out the numbers and vocabulary words listed above in both syllabary and phonetics. Writing them out by hand will strengthen your connection to the words. Speak them aloud. Keep the list handy and make a point of writing the time in Cherokee several times a day. After a while, you won't need to consult your list as often. Since you will be looking at a watch or clock, thinking it through in Cherokee, writing it two ways and pronouncing the words, you won't need to try to memorize anything. Telling time will become second nature before long. If you make Cherokee a part of your daily life rather than something separate that you put away when you close your notebook, you will learn it naturally.

Even though you are starting small and learning, your learning will naturally flow outwards. Follow your curiosity. You may be wondering how you could say the day's date. That will involve learning about ordinal numbers such as 'second,' and 'third,' as well as the months of the year. You will also want to be able to name the day of the week. And when you are learning how to talk about the year or years past, you will be catapulted into a study of large numbers like 'two thousand,' and 'nineteen hundred.'

If you get in the habit of writing the date in Cherokee every morning and reading it aloud, your day will have a Cherokee beginning. Throughout the day, remind yourself of the date, or just the day of the week to carry your Cherokee thinking with you. In that way, you will be lifting Cherokee out of the classroom and textbooks, and making it a part of your own life.

Writing out the day's date and day of the week will help you learn cardinal and ordinal numbers, the names of the months, and how to write out the year. To show you what this could look like, here is today's date and day of the week:

ᎠᏯ ᎢᏓ ᎤᏪᏟᏍᏆᏎ ᏔᎵᏍᎪᎯ ᏐᎭᏁᎵᏁᎢ ᎤᏃᎸᏔᎾ ᎦᎸ ᏔᎵ ᏔᏕᏅᎵ ᏔᎵᏍᎪᎯ ᏔᎵ ᎢᏳᏕᏘᏱᏎᏗᏒᎢ *kohi iga unadodaquidena tal(i)sgohi so/h/nelinei unolvtana kalv tali iyagayvli tal(i)sgohi tali iyudetiyisadisvi*, 'Today is Saturday, the 29th of January, 2022.'

It looks complicated, but it is very manageable when broken down into its component parts:

ᎠᏯ ᎢᏓ *kohi iga*, 'today'

ᎤᏪᏟᏍᏆᏎ *unadodaquidena*, 'Saturday'

ᏔᎵᏍᎪᎯ ᏐᎭᏁᎵᏁᎢ *tal(i)sgohi so/h/nelinei*, '29th'

ᎤᏃᎸᏔᎾ *unolvtana*, 'January'

ᎦᎸ *kalv*, 'the month of'

ᏔᎵ ᏔᏕᏅᎵ ᏔᎵᏍᎪᎯ ᏔᎵ *tali iyagayvli tal(i)sgohi tali*, '2022'

ᎢᏳᏕᏘᏱᏎᏗᏒᎢ *iyudetiyisadisvi*, 'the year of'

Only the day of the week and the date will change every day. You will be writing each month for around thirty days, and you will have three hundred and sixty-five days to practice writing the same year. Changing to the next year on January first should be smooth sailing. If you write the date every day, you will become familiar with all the vocabulary involved, and it will become part of your routine. You will be learning by using the language. No memorization needed.

We naturally remember things which are personal to us because they matter. We all know our own birthdays, and most of us look forward to celebrating each year. Writing out your birthday in Cherokee and taping it to your wall practically guarantees that you will remember that month, day and year in Cherokee. Think also of important people in your life: your family members, close friends, teachers and other role models. Write their birthdays too. You will soon find you are learning a number of different months, ordinal numbers, and how to write different years.

Always remember you are learning the language of the Cherokee people who have a rich history. To help you put your learning into a cultural context, look up the birthdates of famous Cherokees like Sequoyah, Ned Christie, Wilma Mankiller, and Will Rogers. Write down whatever birthdate information you find in Cherokee, even if it is only the year. To make your search even more memorable, look up Cherokees that you admire for a particular reason. If you are interested in archery, for example, you might look up Joe Thornton. If your interest is in mathematics or science, you could look up Mary Golda Ross. Aside from finding out their birthdays, take this opportunity to read about Cherokees you admire. Write out their names and birthdays on cards and post them around your house, as a way of honoring their accomplishments. This connects the words you learn to your heart as well as to your mind. No amount of memorization can do that.

Once you start becoming familiar with numbers, you will notice similarities in groups of numbers, for example the *-i* ending on numbers one through seven: ᎠᏟ *tali*, 'two'; ᏦᎢ *tsoi*, 'three'; ᏅᎩ *nvgi*, 'four'; ᎯᏍᎩ *hisgi*, 'five'; ᏑᏓᎵ *sudali*, 'six'; and ᎦᏟᏉᎩ *ga/h/l(i)-quogi*, 'seven.' You will also notice the *-adu* ending on numbers eleven to nineteen: ᏌᏚ *sadu*, 'eleven'; ᏔᎵᏚ *tal(i)du*, 'twelve'; ᏦᎦᏚ *tsogadu*, 'thirteen'; ᏂᎦᏚ *nigadu*, 'fourteen'; ᏍᎩᎦᏚ *sgigadu*, 'fifteen'; ᏓᎳᏚ *daladu*, 'sixteen'; ᎦᎵᏆᏚ *ga/h/l(i)quadu*, 'seventeen'; ᏁᎳᏚ *neladu*, 'eighteen'; and ᏐᏁᎳᏚ *so/h/neladu*, 'nineteen.' Picturing words grouped by what they have in common, such as common endings, will help cement them in your memory. Keep in mind that although counting up from one in Cherokee is good practice, if you rely on learning the numbers in order only, you will be easily thrown off if you encounter them out of sequence. If you learn to recognize numbers on their own, as you would when writing birthdays, for example, you will recall them without having to see them in order.

With just the addition of a few words, you can use numbers, days and months in your own sentences. For example, if you know that ᎪᎯ ᎢᎦ *kohi iga* is 'today,' ᏌᎾᎴ *sanale*, (or ᏑᎾᎴ *sunale*) means 'tomorrow,' and ᎨᏎᏍᏗ *gesesdi* means 'it will be,' then you can say:

ᎪᎯ ᎢᎦ ᎤᎾᏙᏓᏉᏅ *kohi iga unadodaquo/h/nv*, 'Today is Monday.'

ᏌᎾᎴ ᏔᎵᏁ ᎢᎦ ᎨᏎᏍᏗ *sanale taline iga gesesdi*, 'Tomorrow will be Tuesday.'

You can use the same format to say the day of the month, using ordinal numbers.

ᎪᎯ ᎢᎦ ᏑᏓᎵᏁ *kohi iga sudaline*, 'Today is the sixth.'

ᏌᎾᎴ ᎦᎵᏉᎩᏁ ᎨᏎᏍᏗ *sanale ga/h/l(i)quogine gesesdi*, 'Tomorrow will be the seventh.'

Learning numbers is not difficult at all and it can help you make Cherokee a part of your daily routine.

Using greetings can be another great way to learn Cherokee naturally. Most beginning students learn greetings right away, but may not find opportunities to practice. If you have someone willing to help, you can write greetings on individual cards: person one says ᏏᏲ ᏙᎯᏧ *siyo tohitsu*, 'Hi, how are you?'; person two says ᎣᏍᏓ ᏂᎲᎾ *osda nihina*, 'Fine, and you?'; person one says ᎣᏍᏓ ᏩᏙ *osda wado*, 'Fine, thank you.' Practice, then switch parts. If you have no one with whom to practice, enlist a dog, cat, teddy bear, or even a pillow. You might have to read their parts for them, but I think they will cooperate. At least the teddy bear and the pillow, for certain. Have fun with it. You can also talk to yourself in the mirror. One major benefit is that the person facing you will likely be very sympathetic and patient. And a very good listener.

If you are fortunate enough to have Cherokee speakers in your family or to live in an area where you might run into speakers, don't be afraid to speak Cherokee. Most speakers appreciate people learning the language, and will respond positively when you say ᏏᏲ *siyo*, 'Hi.' It doesn't matter if that's all you can say at first. Speaking even a few words will make you feel like you are a part of the language. Speak Cherokee whenever and wherever you can. For a while, I was a regular at a local coffee shop. I got to know the people working there, and one day decided to greet them with ᏏᏲ *siyo*, 'Hi.' Several workers were interested and they began greeting me with ᏏᏲ *siyo* as soon as I walked in. Later on, a cashier asked me to write ᏏᏲ *siyo* for her, then another asked how to say 'thank you' in Cherokee. I felt at home using the language. Everyone can use Cherokee where they live, even if there are no Cherokee speakers in their area. Bring Cherokee to your own community and you might be surprised how people react. You might even inspire someone to begin their own study of Cherokee.

Another way to begin learning Cherokee is to use weather words. The weather is something that changes day to day, and is particular to where you live. There are beautiful weather posters on the Cherokee Nation website (https://language.cherokee.org/

posters/), which go from very basic weather terms like *rain* and *snow*, to very detailed weather terms like *nimbostratus clouds* and *misting rain*. You can start with just a few weather words that you can write out and keep on your desk. Use the Cherokee Nation posters or the dictionary for a reference. Below are a few common weather terms:

ᎠᎦᏍᎦ ᎠᎦᎵᎭ ᎤᎶᎩᎳ ᎦᏃᎸᎥᏍᎦ ᎫᏘᎭ

agasga *agaliha* *ulogila* *ganolvvsga* *gutiha*

'it is raining' 'the sun is shining' 'it is cloudy' 'the wind is blowing' 'it is snowing'

If you look out your window and see rain, think in Cherokee and say *agasga*. Then write it down in syllabary: ᎠᎦᏍᎦ. You will be learning vocabulary and syllabary at the same time. Look outside again and repeat the word. That will help reinforce your learning, and it will help you to associate *agasga* with actual rain, rather than with the English word 'rain.' Note the outdoor temperature also, and you will have found another way to use number words, and make them part of your life. Then you can write out a daily weather report. It might be something like this:

ᎪᎯ ᎢᎦ ᎠᎦᎵᎭ ᎠᎴ ᏁᎳᏍᎪᎯ ᏄᎵᏌᎳᏓ

kohi iga agaliha ale nel(a)sgohi nul(i)salada.

today sun is shining and 80 it is up to

'It's sunny today and up to 80.'

If you have a friend studying Cherokee who lives in another town or even across the country or world, suggest regularly trading weather reports. You could text or email each other, post on social media, or talk on the phone. That way, you will both have practice observing, writing and then reading about the weather. You might even record weather report videos and send them to one another. Working together makes learning Cherokee more fun.

Learning numbers, dates, conversation and weather vocabulary involves using the words in real-world situations, rather than memorizing from a list. If Cherokee words are attached to your own experience, then you will begin to think in Cherokee. If something is meaningful to you, you will remember it. It only takes a few simple steps like the ones I've outlined to gain confidence and to create a foundation for further learning.

◆ ◆ ◆

Cherokee is a beautiful language, but it takes time to be able to listen and understand, and to speak. One thing students need to be aware of is that in Cherokee the patterns of sounds, or tone and cadence, are very important. There are six vowels in Cherokee, *a, e, i, o, u* and *v*. Each vowel in a word will have a particular tone and cadence. Tone refers to the pitch, or the movement up or down of the voice. There are four pitch levels in Cherokee, and six different patterns are possible with these tones. Cadence, on the other hand, refers just to the length, or duration, of the vowels.

Tone and cadence are essential in Cherokee. Native speakers have learned the language orally, and know tone and cadence intuitively. But second-language learners need to be aware of sound patterns. The *Cherokee-English Dictionary* is very helpful in this regard and indicates the tones with numbers. Numbers written above the vowels give important clues to pronunciation. For example, a pair of numbers can indicate a rise or a fall in the voice: a^{32} shows a falling tone, while a^{23} indicates a rising tone. Vowels at the end of words are naturally short, but other short vowels are indicated with a dot beneath the vowel.

Learners may wonder why tone and cadence are so important. In Cherokee, they are an essential part of the word, and help convey meaning. If you look up DᎣ *ama*, you will find two separate entries for the same spelling, but the tone and cadence will be different: DᎣ *a²ma*, 'water,' and DᎣ *a³ma*, 'salt.' If you wanted to ask for water, but instead pronounced DᎣ *ama* as 'salt,' you might have to wait for a sudden downpour to quench your thirst. This is just one example to show how important sound patterns are.

A good way to understand tone and cadence more deeply is to listen to an audio recording of a word then compare it to the dictionary entry. You'll be able to hear the word and see it represented with markings at the same time.

Learning about tone and cadence is very valuable, but learning the sounds of Cherokee through listening is ideal. Not only will you get a feel for the sound patterns of the words, but you will begin to understand what you hear in context.

Taking classes with a speaker like Ed Fields is a great way to improve your ear for the language. Not long after I started learning, I noticed that Ed would speak in Cherokee at the beginning of class before starting the lesson. Sometimes he would talk about the weather or the date. Sometimes he translated what he had said for the class, and sometimes he didn't. I found it almost impossible to understand what he was saying at those times, but I was determined to find a way to improve my listening. He was giving us a taste of natural speech, speaking as if he were speaking to other Cherokees. And it sounded absolutely beautiful. Wow. I knew this was a unique opportunity. It was up to the students to make the effort to understand—if we wanted to.

I decided I would go back and listen to the recorded classes in the archives. I would play the first few minutes of Ed talking over and over until I could catch a word. And I do mean over and over. It was slow going at first. I wrote down what I heard. I wasn't instantly successful. It seems funny now, but I wasn't able to tell where one word ended and another began. I might write down something like 'cosnel,' only to realize much later that it was *kohi sanale*, 'this morning.' Sometimes I would listen ten times or more before I could sorta-maybe-almost catch a word. That may not sound encouraging, but it was thrilling to me. Did I really just hear Ed say SZꝪiꝏS *ganolvvsga* 'It is windy'? What? I actually understood a word? To hear and understand a word as it was spoken conversationally made me feel, just for a brief moment, that I was standing in the Cherokee world.

I had to work at listening. Hearing a word carefully pronounced in a lesson is very different from being able to pick it out of speech at normal speed. It was a real challenge, but I soon found that my persistence was paying off. I began to be able to pick out a few words at the beginning of class. Then a few more. Over time my listening improved a lot. It took patience and determination, but anyone with patience and determination can do the same. Listen to recordings of Cherokee, wherever you can find them. If you take online classes, listen to the archives as I did. If you have a lesson book with audio, use the recordings and follow along, then listen to the audio without the book. Keep at it until you understand everything just by listening alone. You can also find many Cherokee language videos online, some with captions. Listen and pick out any words you recognize, and try to write down words that you don't know. Paying close enough attention so that you can write the sounds will help you hear more words each time.

◆   ◆   ◆

Patience will help anyone coming face to face with Cherokee verbs for the first time. Cherokee verbs can be packed with a tremendous amount of information. They can tell about an action, and specify how many people are involved, who is doing what to whom, when the action takes place, if a person or animal that is being talked about is facing away from the speaker, if the action is being done repeatedly, if the person who is speaking witnessed the action or not, and much more. And all in one word. That's a lot of information to absorb. It's not suprising that Cherokee learners run screaming from their desks from time to time. But thankfully, no one needs to learn everything all at once. If you work small, and learn a few things very well, you will be laying the groundwork for deeper understanding in the future.

As a long-time attendee in Ed Fields' classes, I am often asked for help outside of class by other students. I've found that when students ask me questions about a topic, I can't assume that they know grammatical terms. I have to formulate a simple and clear explanation, one that anyone can understand and, in doing so, I often find that my own understanding of the topic improves.

In studying Cherokee grammar, you will come across many terms by different authors—*pronominal prefixes, directionals, number inflection, reflexive, verb stems,* and *theme suffixes,* among others. It is important for all of us who are second-language learners to become familiar with grammar. Knowing basic grammar rules helps us to understand phrases we come across, and helps us to create new phrases by applying those rules in different situations. But looking at grammar rules will not help if you don't clearly understand what is being said. When reading about the language, you must first make sure that you understand the terms the author is using. Think about what each term you come across means, and make sure that you understand it well enough to teach it to someone else.

To show you how this would work, begin with a simple Cherokee word ᏥᏬᏂᎭ *tsiwoniha,* 'I am speaking.' You can ask yourself, how does it mean what it means? You might find a simple grammatical explanation like this:

tsiwoniha:
tsiwoniha is a verb which means, 'I am speaking.'
tsi- is a first person singular pronominal prefix
-wonih- is the verb stem
-a is the present continuous suffix

In order to thoroughly understand what is being said, you have to understand the terminology, and since different authors may have different ways of describing the verb, it's important that you know what all the terms refer to. If you don't understand them, you will have gaps in your knowledge going forward. Most texts you use will have glossaries or explanations of terminology used. Although it's tempting to skip over the lists of terms, it will help you if you make yourself familiar with the terms in the beginning.

Consider the phrase, *first person singular pronominal prefix*. Begin with *first person singular,* and if you already know what it means write it down without using any grammatical terms. You can use diagrams, pictures or just words. If you are not sure, look up the term or ask a knowledgeable friend. In grammar, *person* refers to the one doing the action in a sentence. For example, in the sentence, 'I am running,' it is clear that I am doing the action. 'I' would be first person, and it is singular since no one else is included.

The next term to look into is *pronominal*. If you are familiar with the term, write down its meaning in your own words. If you don't know, look up the word in your grammar text or dictionary. You will find that pronominal refers to pronouns, which are words like *I, you, we, he, she,* and *they*. If you search *pronoun prefixes* in a book on Cherokee grammar, you will find that the pronoun prefix is attached in front of the verb stem, and tells who is doing the action. In your own words, write down what a *pronoun prefix* is.

Go through the same process with *verb stem*. You will find that the verb stem tells what the action of the verb is, for example, 'running,' 'speaking,' 'catching.' It also indicates how the action is being done, for example, 'continuously' or in an 'ongoing' way. A prefix attaches to the front of the verb stem, and a suffix, which tells when the action occurs, attaches to the end of the stem. Write a simple definition of *verb stem*.

Last of all, look at the term *present continuous suffix*. You will find that this suffix attaches to the end of the verb stem and shows that the action of the verb is happening in the present moment.

Write what *present continuous suffix* means to you. It's important to write down your understanding of all the terms you have looked up in your own words. Make your definitions as simple as you can.

Now that you understand all the terms being used, write a very simple explanation of how *tsiwoniha* is equivalent to 'I am speaking.' How does the word mean what it means? Can you explain it in easily understood words to another person, without using the grammatical terms? Try explaining it to someone who knows nothing about Cherokee. If you haven't come up with a clear enough explanation, go back and simplify some more. Keep working until it is as simple as you can make it. Your explanation could look something like this:

tsiwoniha is a word that talks about an action

tsi- is placed in front and shows that I am the one doing the action

-wonih- tells that speaking is what is being done, and it is ongoing

-a goes at the end of the word and shows that speaking is being done now.

tsiwoniha is a word that says: I am speaking.

Everything has been covered. By going through these steps, you have made sure that you understand the basic concepts that you will need in order to learn more about verbs. You have understood the linguistic terms. It is very important to be able to read and understand texts dealing with Cherokee grammar. When you have thought about the terms and put them into your own words, you will have real understanding, and will be able to apply what you have learned to other words in Cherokee. Approach everything as if you had to explain it to someone else. Write out your explanations in a notebook and refer back to them. When you have a question later, you will be able to go back quickly and refresh your memory with an explanation you have written yourself. (For more in-depth information on Cherokee verbs see Chapter Six).

This is just one example of how you might study something deeply. You needn't go through this process for everything since you will be building your knowledge base over time. But this process will help you learn more thoroughly.

You will always enjoy studying Cherokee if you delve into what interests you at the moment. At one point, after I had taken all three levels of Ed's classes, I found that there was confusion in my mind about certain verbs having to do with 'going.' Some of them looked very similar. Some seemed to have almost the same meaning, yet they looked different. I had learned the meanings of the words, but I didn't really know how the words meant what they did. I decided to go through each lesson and identify all the words about 'going' that I had questions about. What was the third person (he, she or it) present tense form of the verb? Why was a verb ending that looked like remote past being used for something in the future? Ed was always saying, 'Study the words.' I thought it was time to put that in action, so I wrote out the words I didn't thoroughly understand. My list contained fifteen words like ᎦᏩᏓᏍᏗ *waquedasdi,* 'I have to go over there,' and ᎤᏪᏅᏒ *uwenvsv,* 'He or she went.' I knew the translation of the words, but I wasn't sure if they were related.

My notes would look crazy to anyone else, but were meaningful to me. I wrote out all the words on blank paper, two words per page. I included the words, the lesson sentences and the meanings. I spent about ten days studying these words, distinguishing one from another. Since many of the words were not in the he/she/it form, which is the form used to list verbs in Durbin Feeling's *Cherokee-English Dictionary,* my first goal was to identify that form. That was an education in itself. I spent a lot of time gathering examples from the dictionary of words in Cherokee that had to do with 'going,' and then I looked for similarities to words written on my list. Once I found the third-person form of the verb, I could look up the dictionary entry. This gave me enough information about the verb to begin to understand it. I also paid close attention to the sentence examples in the dictionary for each word, which helped me to understand each word in context. That way, I could create my own similar sentences using the dictionary sentences along with the original sentences from Ed's classes.

Beneath each word I wrote out whatever I understood about the verb, drawing diagrams at times. I worked hard at it. The truth is, I was burning to understand these verbs. No one assigned the work to me. It wasn't an exercise from a book. It was something that required concentration and persistence, but I was motivated by my own desire to understand the language. I didn't stop until I had accomplished all I had set out to do. That's not to say I had learned everything there was to know about those words. But I had learned as much as I could at the time. Later, I would find additional examples of how the words were used, and other related words to expand my understanding even more.

I could easily supply my list and all my notes, or even just the third-person singular form of the verbs I studied, but that would be robbing readers of the opportunity to research and learn on their own. Write down words that you are unsure of. Maybe you heard them in a Cherokee language classroom. Maybe you read them in a lesson book, or just saw them online. You might want to make a list of words that talk about 'going,' as I did. Whatever words you want to understand, work to uncover the answers yourself, if possible. Finding one thing out on your own is worth more than twenty answers handed to you.

Whatever it is that captures your interest—it could be a word that your teacher mentions in class or something you read—follow it up. Study whatever you feel passionate about at the moment. Feed that fire, and you will never be bored studying Cherokee. And whenever you study anything in depth, it will carry over to everything else you are learning.

Make it a point to understand what you are studying well enough to be able to explain it to someone else. If you are studying how to talk about the future in Cherokee, write down what you learn in simple terms, using drawings if you like. That way, you will have something easily understandable to refer back to when you run into the future tenses again, and you will also be able to explain them to other students. Over time, your knowledge will grow, and you may revise what you wrote and add additional examples. In this way, you will be creating your own language reference booklet, and by choosing what you want to study, you will be handcrafting your own course of study.

◆　◆　◆

If you want to be truly well-rounded in the Cherokee language, you will want to learn to read and write syllabary. The Cherokee syllabary is the invention of one incredible, dedicated Cherokee silversmith, Sequoyah, also known as George Guess or George Gist. Beginning around 1809, he worked tirelessly to devise a writing system, believing that the ability to communicate through writing would help the Cherokee people. By the late 1820s, his syllabary, as we know it today, was complete: eighty-five characters which included six vowels, the *s* sound, and complete syllables made up of both a consonant and a vowel. It was a work of genius. Cherokee people quickly embraced the new writing system. Here is a quote from a man who visited among the Cherokees in 1828 from the *American Annals of Education and Instruction, For the Year 1832*, Vol II:

'When I travelled through the Cherokee Nation, during the months of January and February, 1828, before the press was set up, or any printing had been executed in the alphabet of Guess, I was informed in many parts of the nation, that almost all the young and middle aged men could read in that alphabet, with many of the old men, and of the women, and of the children . . . I frequently saw, as I rode from place to place, Cherokee letters painted or cut on the trees by the road side, on fences, houses, and often on pieces of bark or board, lying about the houses. The alphabet of Guess had never been taught in schools. The people have learned it from one another; and that too without books, or paper, or any of the common facilities for writing or teaching. They cut the letters, or drew them with a piece of coal, or with paint. Bark, trees, fences, the walls of houses, &c. answered the purpose of paper or slates. That the mass of a people, without schools or books, should by mutual assistance, without extraneous impulse or aid, acquire the art of reading, and that in a character wholly original, is, I believe, a phenomenon unexampled in modern times.' [1]

The Cherokee people worked cooperatively to learn the syllabary because it mattered to them. Writing to relatives west of the Mississippi mattered to them. Sharing information and news, when Removal was being talked of, mattered to them. It mattered to them not only as individuals, but also as a people who wanted control over their future. They felt a sense of urgency and helped one another learn. Now, 200 years after Sequoyah invented the syllabary, there is a renewed urgency to learn. The Cherokee language is, at this very moment, on the verge of dying out. Within two generations it will be spoken, read, written and taught only by second-language learners, unless new learners teach their children in their homes. This is a heartbreaking reality. But all learners can help keep the language alive by learning, and that includes learning syllabary.

Students may sometimes think there is no real need to learn syllabary, since phonetics are widely used. Phonetics are important, and very useful to second-language learners, but they are not authentically Cherokee. Phonetics show Cherokee sounds in relationship to the English alphabet. But Cherokees worked together to learn Sequoyah's syllabary, not an English phonetic version. If you are writing syllabary, you are writing the same characters that Cherokee learners wrote from the 1820s on. If you are reading aloud from the syllabary, you are doing what many Cherokees did to share news from the *Cherokee Phoenix*, or a letter from relatives in Arkansas territory. Reading and writing syllabary shows solidarity with those who came before. When you learn syllabary you are telling the world that the Cherokee writing system still matters and is still worth preserving.

Learning the syllabary will require determination, but it is worth the effort. There are various books and methods that can help you get started. There are also groups on social media that will encourage and help all learners. People learn differently, and what worked for one may not be right for another. But I can share that after trying memorization, at which I failed miserably, I came across the book *Simply Cherokee: Let's Learn Cherokee Syllabary* by Marc W. Case. It associated the shapes of the letters with brief stories. For example, the character Ꮡ *su* was taught with a brief story about a girl named Sue whose curly hair looked like the Cherokee character.[2] That worked well for me, perhaps because I am a very visual person. I became familiar with the characters very quickly, but I realized that I would have to practice in order to keep them in my memory. Every day, for just a few minutes, I would open the *Cherokee-English Dictionary*. I looked at random syllabary entries, covering the phonetics at the same time, and sounded out the characters. I was a real beginner and understood very few words in the dictionary, but that didn't matter. My goal was to be able to recognize syllabary. There were plenty of times when I would make mistakes. I wasn't concerned about that. I would go back to the syllabary chart and refresh my memory. I would also write out syllabary words from the dictionary for writing practice.

I particularly liked the sample sentences in the dictionary. I enjoyed being able to write down real, meaningful phrases. That made me feel like I was really using the language. Even if I understood very little, I was able to see how sentences were put together. Also, some of the sentences really caught my interest. I remember finding this sentence in the *Cherokee-English Dictionary*: "ᏚᏴᎳᏓ ᏤᏍᎤᏗ ᏤᎥᏍᎥ

ShᎯᎥᎢᎫ DhᏣᏪᎩ, *Jugidahli diganhdi dikwsdo dunilvkwdi Anijalagi,* 'Cherokees like feather pillows.'" [3] I thought that was amusing. And it also made me think of a feather pillow I had when I was a child. So, I felt personally connected to the words in the sample sentence, and would go back and look at it from time to time. I was practicing syllabary, but learning so much more. Before long, my syllabary recognition improved. I could write lesson words in syllabary, and any words I found in the dictionary. Learning to read Cherokee syllabary made me feel I was continuing a process that had begun two hundred years before. Every student can learn. One student might find it's a slow gradual process. Another might learn more quickly. It doesn't matter. If you care enough to try, you will succeed.

When you are learning syllabary, it's important to write by hand. It's fun to type in syllabary, and it's a good way to use Cherokee on your phone or computer with friends. But typing has its limitations. When you touch a screen or type on a keyboard, there is no direct connection between your hand movements and the shape of the character that appears on the screen. But when you write the words yourself, your hand, finger and arm muscles are actually all involved in forming the letters. You are also using your eyes to guide your hand, and if you say what you write as well, you will hear the sound of the characters as they are being written. The process uses different parts of your brain together, which helps you to remember.

Once you have learned how to form the characters, you may want to practice and refine your handwriting. Syllabary writing can be very beautiful. If you'd like to see how syllabary was written in the past, you can find examples of old, original Cherokee writing at the *Digital Archive of American Indian Languages Persistence* (https://dailp.northeastern.edu/). The site serves as a digital archive, preserving old documents handwritten in Cherokee. Each of the documents is presented in several different views, offering translations, analysis, word breakdown and audio, as well as a scan of the original handwritten document. This allows everyone, even beginning learners, access to old documents, and provides different models for Cherokee syllabary handwriting.

One set of documents may be of particular interest to those learning to write syllabary. The "Dollie Duncan Letters" are a collection of letters written from a young man in prison to his mother. Since he was still learning to write, a fellow prisoner wrote most of the letters for him. His friend's handwriting was very beautiful, and it seems he took great pride in writing in syllabary. Looking at his writing, one can imagine him slowly and carefully forming each character. Such examples of handwriting show that Cherokee characters are not connected to one another as they are in English cursive. Some of the characters take several strokes to complete, such as Ꮓ *hna*, while others may be written with one continuous flowing line, such as Ꮺ *we*. It's almost as if the syllabary characters themselves were telling you not to hurry, but to enjoy the process of communication in Cherokee. Copying words by hand from the scan of an original document will help you feel more connected to the history of Cherokee writing.[4]

If you see beauty in the Cherokee syllabary and beauty in the precision of the language, that is probably enough reason for you to want to learn the language. If you have the opportunity, take a class from a native speaker. Teachers like Ed give so generously of their time, and you will gain a perspective and understanding that can't be found in books alone. There have been so many times I've been inspired by what Ed has said in classes, and have researched words and phrases that struck a chord with me. A good teacher should light a fire that illuminates the language so brightly that students can't help but want to learn more, even beyond the classroom. Ed Fields does that.

However you learn, remember to begin small and use the language in your everyday life. That way you will be living the language, rather than just studying it. And remember that the language needs new speakers to carry the language into the future, and there's plenty of room on the pathway. If I can learn, so can you.

CHAPTER FIVE

How is Cherokee Different

From English?

ED FIELDS

ᏏᏲ ᏂᎦᏛ *siyo nigadv*, 'Hello, all of you,' I'm glad you're here. Over the years some students and people have commented on or asked questions about some of the differences between Cherokee and English. So I will talk about some of the differences, and also some of the similarities. I hope this helps you.

Maybe one of the first differences they comment on is that 'the Cherokee alphabet is different than the English alphabet.' ii *vv*, 'Yes,' the Cherokee syllabary is different than the English alphabet. Once you see the differences it can help you in your learning of the Cherokee language.

An alphabet is made up of characters that have sounds, you put the sounds together to form syllables, then you use these syllables to form words. You learn the characters and sounds for the English alphabet and learn how to make words with them.

A syllabary is made up of characters that have sounds, these sounds are already put together for you to form syllables. (See, the Cherokee language actually saves you a learning-step since the syllables are already put together for you.) Then you use these syllables to form words. You learn the characters and the sounds for the Cherokee syllabary and learn how to make words with them.

The English alphabet and the Cherokee syllabary both have sounds, some different and some similar. And they both have characters, many different and some similar. So, great news, you already know many of the Cherokee syllabary sounds. And, more great news, you already know how to write some Cherokee characters. See how far you are ahead in your Cherokee journey already.

But these similarities and differences can also make it a challenge in the beginning of your Cherokee journey. Because a learner may look at the Cherokee word ᏪᏌ *wesa* but tend to pronounce the sounds like their first-language brain has been trained to do, with the English pronunciations.

Just give yourself time. Give your brain time to learn the other way of saying these sounds, the Cherokee language way, and you will learn. And over time, you'll be able to switch from the English pronunciations to the Cherokee pronunciations and back again easier and easier. What will help you in this part of the journey is to stop thinking of it as a Cherokee alphabet and begin to think of it as a Cherokee syllabary. Thinking of it as an alphabet sets you up for struggles. Because the thinking and reasoning needed to learn and walk about in a syllabary is different from that needed to learn and walk about in an alphabet. So help yourself take a big step forward in your learning today by starting to think syllabary, not alphabet. Tell yourself, 'I am learning a syllabary language.'

If that is not one of the first differences that new learners notice, then they notice the Cherokee syllabary has some characters that look like some characters in the English alphabet (T, D, etc.). This can confuse beginning learners because they may be expecting those syllabary characters to sound like the English alphabet characters. For example, they may be expecting T to sound like 'tuh' and D like 'duh.' Instead, they are pronounced like the Cherokee syllabary has them. Most Cherokee syllabary charts list the sounds represented for you. In the beginning of your learning, the alphabet-looking characters used in the syllabary may confuse you, but over time you'll be less and less confused. Just give your brain time to learn the new system and make the new connections. And you'll do just fine.

These things are just normal in learning a language. If you stop thinking of them as being abnormal or hard or difficult, then you'll help yourself. Just think of them as something that is to be learned and go on from there, learning and continuing to learn.

Another difference beginning learners notice is that at the top of the Cherokee syllabary chart there are some vowel sounds that seem to be represented by the English alphabetic characters for English vowels—*a, e, i, o, u*—and there is a *v* which may make some think it sounds like the English 'v.' These English alphabetic characters may make the English speaker's brain sometime revert to thinking in English instead of in Cherokee. When they see the character '*i*' their brain, which has been trained to think and reason in the English language, may think English vowel 'i' sound when in fact it is a Cherokee '*e*' sound. And when they see the character '*e*' their brain may think English vowel 'e' sound when in fact it is a Cherokee '*eh*' sound (pronounced like an old man who has a hard time hearing and he says '*Eh?*').

This new way of vowel thinking and speaking may be confusing in the beginning of your journey into the Cherokee language, but over time it gets less and less so. Just like when learning any language. Just continue to train your brain to the new and you will learn. Just give your brain time to adjust and learn, to make the new connections and corrections. If frustrated, remember to slow down and enjoy the journey. You'll get there.

When learning the Cherokee syllabary chart, it may help you to think of the syllabary chart as 'The Six Grandpas And Their Family Members.' The top row of the chart has the vowels, there are six vowels or six governing sounds, or you can look at them like they are six grandpas. The six grandpas have names, vowel names. And each grandpa has a column that they govern, that are relatives. These top row sounds are grandpas and below them in the column

Table 5.1 The Six Grandpas

The Six Grandpas and their Families					
D a	R e	T i	ꮼ o	Ꭴ u	i v
S ga ꮣ ka	Ᏽ ge/ke	Ᏸ gi/ki	A go/ko	J gu/ku	E gv/kv
Ᏺ ha	P he	ꭸ hi	Ꮉ ho	Γ hu	Ꮂ hv
W la	Ꮭ le	Ꮅ li	G lo	M lu	Ꮑ lv
ꮉ ma	Oᏽ me	H mi	ꮞ mo	Ᏽ mu	Ꮇ mv
Θ na Ꮭ hna Ꮕ nah	Ꮑ ne/hne	h ni/hni	Z no/hno	Ꮔ nu/hnu	OᏌ nv/hnv
Ꮖ qua	ꮖ que	Ᏼ qui	Ꮖ quo	ꮗ quu	Ꮄ quv
Ꮑ sa ꮝ s	4 se	b si	Ꮢ so	ꮞ su	R sv
Ꮭ da Ꮤ ta	S de Ꮟ te	Ꭿ di Ꭴ ti	V do/to	S du/tu	ꮫ dv/tv
ꮪ dla Ꮮ tla	L tle/dle	C tli/dli	ꮶ tlo/dlo	Ꮧ tlu/dlu P tlv/dlv	
G tsa	V tse	Ᏼ tsi	K tso	ꮪ tsu	Ꮳ tsv
Ꮆ wa/hwa	ꮕ we/hwe	Ꮕ wi/hwi	Ꮼ wo/hwo	Ꮽ wu/hwu	6 wv/hwv
ꮿ ya/hya	Ᏸ ye/hye	ꮾ yi/hyi	Ꮀ yo/hyo	G yu/hyu	B yv/hyv

*Beloved s to all the Grandpas and their families.

these sounds are their relatives. Like their wives, sisters, brothers, sons, daughters, grandchildren and great grandchildren. Just a big syllabary family. If you look at the six grandpas, their names are those six vowel sounds. Their relatives, which are in the column below each of the grandpas, will have their own grandpa's name. Except for ꮝ s. That ꮝ s doesn't have any Grandpas' last name. So you can think of ꮝ s as a very beloved foster-child or adopted relative. And the other family members really love ꮝ s, they really like to get together and spend time with ꮝ s. One Cherokee elder told me that ꮝ s is used a lot, even sometimes more than other syllables. They are all just one big, happy syllabary family.

Now, another difference learners tend to notice is that there are 86 characters in the Cherokee syllabary, but only 26 characters in the English alphabet. This may make them think that Cherokee has a lot, or even too many, characters for them to learn, and that

Cherokee will be hard to learn because they're used to a 26-character alphabet. But stop and think. How many syllables are there to learn in the English alphabet? Compare the number of syllables in the Cherokee syllabary with the number of syllables in the English alphabet *after* you have used the alphabet's 26 characters to make all syllables. How many syllables are there in the English alphabet? Do you think English has fewer or more syllables to learn than Cherokee?

In the online and immersion classes I sometimes give the students a ZⱰb *noqu(i)si*, 'star' when they do a good job or make an advance in their learning or get an important question correct. So if you said 'English has more syllables to learn than Cherokee' then here is your ZⱰb *noqu(i)si*, 'star.' (See Figure 5.1).

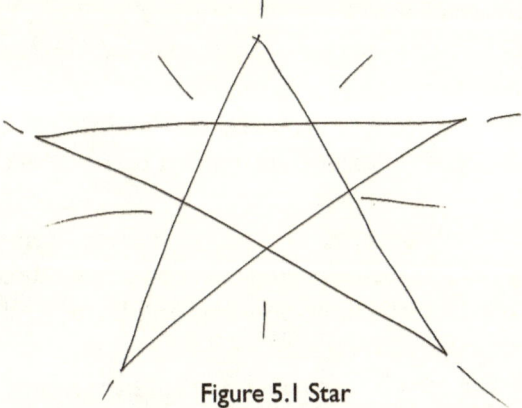

Figure 5.1 Star

So how many syllables are there in the English language? One study says there are over 15,000 while another study says there are over 18,000 syllables. Either is a lot of syllables to learn. Even if you didn't learn all 18,000 or 15,000—even if you just learned a fourth of that—that is still a lot of syllables to learn. As you can see, English has many, many more syllables than Cherokee. And since you had the patience and brain power to learn thousands of English syllables, isn't it reasonable to think that you can learn the lesser amount of Cherokee syllables?

So good news, you don't have to learn several thousands of syllables. You only have to learn the lesser amount of Cherokee syllables. Just give your brain and you time to learn.

But if you're concerned that you can't learn all the sounds in the Cherokee syllabary consider this—you already know many of them. Many of the Cherokee sounds are the same sounds as in English. Look at the sounds represented in the syllabary and compare them to sounds represented by the English alphabet and alphabetical syllables (syllables made after putting English character-sounds together). For instance, if you can make the 's' sound that a snake makes, you already know ꮝ *s* in the Cherokee syllabary. And if you know 'me, myself and I' then you know Ᏽ *mi*. And if you know a cow goes 'moo' then you know Ᏻ *mu*. If you know how to laugh 'ha, ha' then you know Ᏺ *ha*, and 'hee, hee' then you know Ꭿ *hi*, and 'ho, ho, ho' then you know Ᏺ *ho*. And so on. You already know many of the sounds.

Are there going to be some sounds that may be new to you, that you will have to learn? Sure, but not over 18,000 of them or even 15,000 of them or even a fourth of that. Out of the number of Cherokee syllables, you know many already. Remember, it's nothing to be intimidated or frightened of, it's just something for you to give your brain time to process and learn. And time and practice will help you do that.

As you can see Cherokee and English have some differences but also some similarities. When potential new learners are told that Cherokee has no similarities to English at all, it can sometimes intimidate or even scare off some of them. But as you've just seen there are some similarities. Many same sounds that you already know how to produce. Some same character shapes that you already know how to write. And some same syllables that you already know how to pronounce. So you are already that far ahead in your journey into the Cherokee language.

Now, let's look at some other ways Cherokee and English are different, but also similar. And let's have some fun while we do this, because learning ought to be fun, as fun as we can make it, VᎣ *doka*, 'isn't that right?'

Think of the phrase 'that makes my taste-buds sing.' Now, you may be thinking, what's so fun about that? To a Cherokee speaker and elder it can be very funny, because Cherokee is a language that picturizes—pictures things. When I hear 'my taste-buds sing' a picture pops into my mind of taste-buds singing. Not actual human taste-buds, because they wouldn't have mouths to sing and the picturized ones do have mouths. So to me that is a funny picture, taste-buds singing. But my mind tells me 'taste-buds do not sing, they may taste but not sing.' But the picture is funny, to see taste-buds singing is funny.

If you were picturizing taste-buds singing what would they look like? What you picture and how you picture is unique—and uniquely you. And if more Cherokee elders heard the phrase 'my taste-buds sing' imagine what pictures they might picturize! And if you could see what they were picturizing, you might see a whole stage production of different types of singing taste-buds.

This funny (at least to me) story shows another difference between Cherokee and English. English seems to me to be more representative. In English the taste-buds are not really singing. It is a way of representing what the person felt. Cherokee, on the other hand, is precision, picturizing and fact- or truth-based. A Cherokee first-language speaker and elder when hearing the phrase may automatically picture taste-buds singing. Or maybe that's just me. I see in pictures sometimes when someone talks to me in English. Maybe because that is what I do in Cherokee, so it's just natural for me.

Another fun time I want to tell you about was when I was visiting with three people—two Cherokee speakers and one English speaker. One of the Cherokee speakers told the three of us this story.

A man from Arkansas always drives many miles to visit my brother's Oklahoma roadside store once a week. This week the man drove all the miles there, pulled up, got out of his car, looked around, saw this big tree limb on the ground and asked, 'What happened to that big limb?' There had been a storm the night before and the big tree limb was on the ground. And my relative said, 'Turkey fell.' And the man said, 'Boy, that must have been one big bird!'

The three of us Cherokee speakers all laughed, we thought it a very funny story. Also, we knew what had happened, because it had happened to us in similar situations and would probably happen again. But the English speaker smiled vaguely and looked a question at us. The one who had told the story explained.

My relative couldn't recall the English words for 'the limb fell off.' He couldn't think of the English words for what he was trying to say. His Cherokee mind was saying ᎬᎾ ᏍᎦᎸ *gvn(a) galohi*, 'turkey fell,' which is what Cherokees say when a limb is broken off or falls off, so he said the part of that Cherokee phrase that he could translate into English quickly enough for the conversation—'turkey fell.' And the man asking about the limb then thought it was a turkey that landed on the big tree limb, a huge heavy turkey that broke the big limb. That's why he said, 'Boy, that must have been one big bird!'

This time we all laughed.

Both stories, the one about the singing taste-buds and the 'turkey fell,' show me that in the English and Cherokee languages people can find word-play and humor, even with the differences between the languages. Both languages share this similarity. Just think, when you learn Cherokee you'll have two languages you can tell and hear funny stories in. You'll have double the fun.

Sometimes beginning learners notice things that are not so much differences between Cherokee and English as differences between Cherokee dialects. Not just North Carolina and Oklahoma dialects, but community dialects. Sometimes learners want to know 'why are there different Cherokee dialects' and 'which Cherokee dialect is the correct dialect to use.'

You have to remember that Cherokee was orally learned. Way back before Sequoyah invented his syllabary there were no schools for Cherokee children to learn the Cherokee language. There were no schools to teach the children the Cherokee syllabary characters. So there was not one uniform or standardized dialectical sound system for them to teach them to read in Cherokee, to write in Cherokee, to teach them the correct grammar constructions.

Cherokee was orally learned.

Even when I was growing up, the English school I had to go to did not teach in a bilingual type program. The language used was English. This meant the Cherokee language was left to Cherokee families, communities, even regions or counties, to determine the dialects. Families, communities, regions or counties could have their own dialects, their own different ways of pronouncing Cherokee.

Within one family there could be many dialects, many ways of pronouncing Cherokee. For instance, dad may pronounce one way but mom, who came from a different area, pronounced things her way. Grandparents on the mom's side had their ways, each influenced by their different areas. And grandparents on the dad's side had their ways, each influenced by their different areas. And the two-sets of great-grandparents, for a total of four great-grandparents, had their ways, each influenced by their different areas. Then there were the cousins, aunts, uncles, and other family members who had their ways. ii *vv*, 'Yes,' each influenced by their different areas. And then the neighbors had their ways, each influenced by their relatives and different areas. And community members had their ways, each influenced by their relatives and different areas. And town and county members had their ways, each influenced by their relatives and different areas.

Whew, that's a lot of people and a lot of different ways. No wonder there are different dialects or different ways of pronouncing Cherokee.

About the different dialects and which to use, don't let the dialects intimidate you, just pick whichever one or ones you want to use, then learn and use it or them. Cherokee speakers are very versatile, we will be able to understand you. And don't demand Cherokee speakers or even learners speak in one dialect—as in "this is the correct dialect" or "this is the only real Cherokee dialect"—instead allow them their own and the freedom of choice you also have.

I'm not saying you learn in a lax way or lazy way or disrespectful to the language way. Nor am I saying you should support or encourage someone misusing the language. I am thinking you are intelligent enough and respectful enough and caring, compassionate enough that you will know when someone is being disrespectful or even harming the language and you will not use that or speak that or teach that or pass it on. Instead you will know the real words, meanings and dialects and hold to those and support those and speak that and use that and teach that and pass that on.

Another thing learners sometimes find confusing is that the syllabary has some characters that look similar to each other. For instance, W and W, R and R (*la* and *ta*, *e* and *sv*)—these and a few others may seem to look similar to new learners. But again, just say them as you see and write them. If you can, listen to a first-language Cherokee speaker pronounce them and you repeat, and then listen again and repeat but this time also write the syllable. Then look at it, and pronounce it again. With practice and time, you'll learn them and be able to help others learn them too.

Of course, the Cherokee language is written by using syllabary, which is not an alphabet, but some beginning learners want to know 'should I use phonetics or syllabary to write Cherokee?' You may be wondering the same or whether you should use both.

Now, some languages do not have an alphabet or a syllabary, they have phonetics. But when a language does have an alphabet or a syllabary then phonetics is not really the written form of that language, phonetics is the sounds of that written language. When you write the Cherokee language using phonetics you are writing the sounds or sound-alikes of the Cherokee written language. Syllabary is the Cherokee written language.

So, ii *vv*, 'yes,' the Cherokee syllabary is the written form of the Cherokee language. The phonetics is the sounds of that written and spoken language. Each Cherokee language learner will have to decide for themselves which they want to learn to use.

Most Cherokee language learners I've met say they want to show respect to and honor Sequoyah, and they want to show respect to and honor past and present Cherokee elders and ancestors, and to do this they want to write in syllabary or write in both syllabary and phonetics. But as I said, each learner will have to decide for themselves. Do what you need to do in order to learn the Cherokee language, if phonetics help you then write in phonetics until you can write in syllabary. Just remember that when you are using phonetics to write the Cherokee language that you are using the English alphabet, which is not a syllabary (you are learning *wesa* instead of ᏪᏌ). And using the English alphabet to learn the Cherokee language may or may not turn out to be a hindrance to you. If you're an English speaker and reader using phonetics, using English alphabetical characters to represent Cherokee sounds may now and then make your brain revert back to thinking and reasoning in English instead of in Cherokee. It may hinder you or slow your learning progress. So that may be a concern for you.

When an English speaker learns the English alphabet, they learn the alphabetic characters, the ABCs, and they learn the sounds (phonetics) of those characters or letters. But they do not use the sounds (phonetics) to write English words and sentences. They use the alphabetic characters or letters, the ABCs, to write English words and sentences. Learners coming to the Cherokee language need to wean themselves away from using the sounds (phonetics) and allow themselves to grow into using the syllabary.

I tell beginning students and learners in the online and immersion classes to start as soon as possible to learn the syllabary. As early in your journey as you can, learn how to recognize the characters and their sounds so that later on you'll be able to read them. And as early in your journey as you can, learn how to say them and write them. Because sooner or later you'll be using syllabary characters, since if you want to write to other Cherokee learners they may be writing in syllabary or if you're reading in the Cherokee language it's usually in syllabary, especially the old writings of our ancestors. And syllabary writing does save you time and effort as the syllabary characters say a lot in less space than phonetics. Most learners who learn how to read and write in syllabary do so for the Cherokee language and the Cherokee elders and ancestors. To them it is a matter of respect, honor, caring and love. Also, if fewer people use the syllabary, then it dies.

And just think, when you begin learning to read and write the syllabary you'll be writing syllabary characters like they did when Sequoyah taught them hundreds of years ago. Like you, they too took a writing tool in hand and made that first line, that first curve. They too had to learn how to read and write the syllabary.

Remember that you can do it. If you are thinking that learning to read and write in the syllabary is too "hard" or "difficult," take heart, Patrick Del Percio and Mary Rae both learned to read and write in the syllabary. So others have learned it, and you can too. When you're beginning to learn to write in syllabary, just study, practice and give yourself time and you'll write just fine in syllabary or, if you prefer, both phonetics and syllabary.

When you're first learning the syllabary characters, it helps if you say each character out loud as you write it. There is something that happens in your brain when your hand writes, your eyes see, your mouth and tongue say and your ears hear. All these senses focused on learning this one thing at the same time can speed up the learning process. And it may work faster for you and help you retain the learning better than when you just use one or two senses.

You know, sometimes things may seem hard or scary, but you

can do it. Will you make mistakes? Sure, that's how you learn. Just correct the mistakes and go on. And Cherokee learners, for that matter most people, are kind and understanding. Sometimes it is us who are hardest on ourselves and beat ourselves over the head or call ourselves names. You would not treat someone you care about like that, so don't treat yourself like that either.

Sometimes we'll give someone else lots of support and encouragement and cheer them on, but to our self we give almost none—or maybe even none. Instead, learn how to be your own supporter and encourager. Sometimes there are no others around to do that, sometimes you have to do it yourself. Of course, ᎤᏁᏛᎢ ᎠᎴ ᏥᏌ *Unetlanvhi ale Tsisa*, 'Creator, God and Jesus' are always there. But I am talking about people being there. Sometimes we wish we had lots of supportive people in our lives, but life does not always work out that way for various reasons. So learn to be your own supportive person. But do this in a wise and sane way. In Cherokee we lift each other up—ᏕᏣᏓᏌᎳᏗᎮᏍᏗ *detsadasaladihesdi*, 'uplift one another.' Keep doing that. But remember, how can you lift someone else up if you have let yourself fall? So keep climbing, and keep lifting others up.

Well, I'm supposed to be talking about the differences between Cherokee and English but have gotten off on a ᏥᏍᏚ *tsisdu*, 'rabbit' trail, huh?

So, what is another thing that beginning learners notice first? The length of the words, that is, they notice how many syllables are in one word. But really it is not one word, many times it is a whole phrase or sentence.

ᏙᎾᏓᎪᎲᎢ *donadagohvi*.

To a learner just starting out they may think of that "word" as meaning 'good-bye,' because they are just starting and so they are still coming at the Cherokee language from their English language point-of-view. They may think 'six syllables is a lot of syllables to say what a two-syllable English word says when it says good-bye.'

They may even get discouraged because they may think 'if a simple word like 'good-bye' is that long, how much longer are the less simple words!'

But VƟᏞAᎲT *donadagohvi* does not mean 'good-bye.'

VƟᏞAᎲT *donadagohvi* is not one word. It is a complete sentence, so to be fair we should allow it to have more syllables, VᎧ *doka*, 'isn't that right?'

VƟᏞAᎲT *donadagohvi* means 'Let us, you and I, see each other again.' One sentence—six Cherokee syllables. Now that's concise.

Of course, it does not always go like that. Sometimes Cherokee words, phrases and sentences do have more syllables. But the English words, phrases and sentences sometimes do too.

But when you're just starting to learn Cherokee and you see the syllables and there are more than four syllables, you may have trouble with the pronunciation because the English trained mind and tongue are used to pronouncing words of fewer syllables. I've heard that most English words come in one, two, three or four syllables. And each two to four syllable word is spaced a little apart from the other words that come before and after it. Fewer syllables and spaces between each word give the English speaker's mind and tongue a bit of a break and enough of a pause for their brain to catch meanings in the pauses between the words. This is a different language structure than Cherokee. A learner just starting to learn Cherokee has the task of adding an additional skill-set to their mind and tongue—training the mind and tongue to speak more than four syllables in a row and to understand more quickly because they don't have as many pauses between the words.

VƟᏞAᎲT *donadagohvi* has six syllables. When you pronounce VƟᏞAᎲT *donadagohvi* which syllable tries to make your tongue slow down or tries to get it to tangle up just a bit? Is it the fourth or the fifth? If so, you may be used to speaking less than four or five syllables in a row. Learning the Cherokee language will help you master that skill. It is doable. Remember, some of the English language words do have more than four syllables and you have learned to pronounce them.

Don't let the length of a Cherokee "word" or number of syllables make you worried or concerned or fearful. Just give yourself time. Over time, you'll get it. Meanwhile, when pronouncing them, just slow down and let your tongue and mind get used to the syllables, then continue and over time they become natural to you. Sometimes students tell me that they are beginning to dream in Cherokee, and they are very excited about it because they know Cherokee is becoming a part of them. After your tongue and mind get used to the syllables and words, they'll be easier to say and you'll be able to say them faster. It becomes more and more natural to think and speak, even dream, in Cherokee.

What may help is to write them in the Cherokee syllabary as you say them. Remember the more of your senses that you bring to your learning the better and faster you'll learn. Write them as you say them and hear them.

You know, someone told me that some people were saying that learning the Cherokee syllabary actually hinders a learner from learning the Cherokee language. Isn't that odd? No one says that about the English alphabet, which is used to make strange alphabetical spellings (silent b in some words, ph that sounds like f, words that sound alike but are spelled differently, and so many more things) no one seems to say 'don't learn the English alphabet because it'll hinder you from learning English.' Do you think that maybe if people stopped talking about how hard and difficult things are, and instead told people how capable their brains and minds are, then people could find themselves learning Cherokee easier and faster?

I hope you can see that over time it is possible to learn Cherokee, even when you are an adult. You are never too old or too young to learn Cherokee. Also, you can learn the syllabary. Your brain is capable of doing this. You are capable of doing this. The people who are telling you that you cannot do it, don't let them win. Instead of listening to the Ꮭ *tla*, 'no,' just start saying the ii *vv*, 'yes.' ii *vv*, 'Yes,' I can do it.' And give yourself time.

And that is another thing. Have you ever noticed how many years English students get to learn English. Kindergarten to twelfth grade (even longer if including pre-school years and university years). That's thirteen or more *years* for learning English. Yet learners of Cherokee are squeezed into thinking it takes only two or four *semesters* to learn Cherokee. Or, if they're in the online class, they think if they take Cherokee I, then Cherokee II and then Cherokee III for a total of 30 weeks then "it is enough to learn Cherokee," and if they don't know it by the end of 30 weeks then it probably means it was "too hard and difficult" or that they "weren't smart enough" and so "they can't do it." Does this seem fair to you—to expect so little time for a student to learn Cherokee and yet give a student to learn English thirteen or more *years* for learning English.

When you are on your journey into learning the Cherokee language, don't squeeze yourself into such limited time constraints. Give yourself years. And remember, even English speakers are really not limiting themselves to just years, as they are learning for a lifetime because they learn new English words and sayings over their entire lives. Why not give Cherokee fair treatment?

ii *vv*, 'Yes,' I have gone down another ᎤᎾᏍ *tsisdu*, 'rabbit' trail. It is just that I do not like unfair treatment of you. I don't want people treating you unfairly. And I don't want you treating yourself unfairly. *You can do it.* Give yourself a chance and give yourself time.

Now, if you are only wanting to spend a little time, say to learn the syllabary or maybe just a few words to pass on to others, then that is still a help. ᎠᏎᏃ *ase/h/no*, 'But' if you want to spend longer, say having Cherokee in your life your whole life long, then begin to think that way, to program your brain for that. To just rest and relax into the idea of you learning Cherokee your whole life long. Just accept it and let the pressure and stress fall away—you're not limited to ten weeks of learning or two semesters, or four semesters, etc., instead you're unlimited by those time-frames. You'll be learning new words, or maybe some of the old ones too, all your life long. And then just do it. Like me and Meli (Mary) and others who are walking in Cherokee for our lifetimes, you'll be a Cherokee lifetime learner too. So, 'welcome to the Cherokee lifetime learners,' *detsvdanilvgv tsalagi dotsadeloquasgi igohidv otsehvi* (see Figure 5.2).

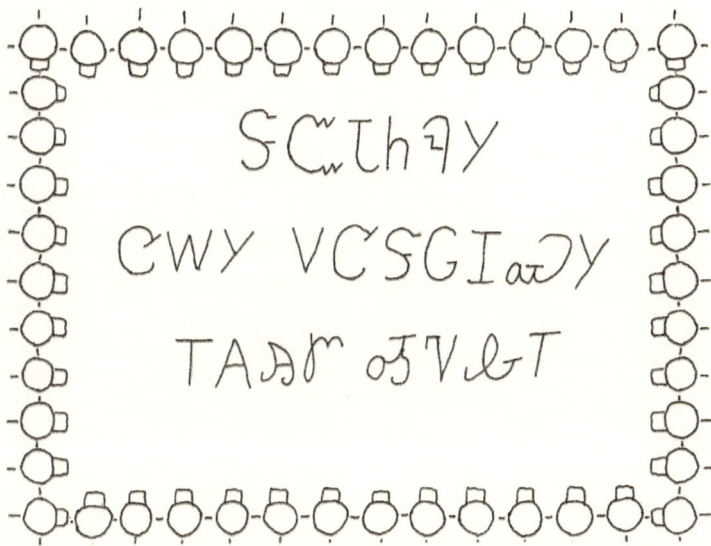

Figure 5.2. Lighted Sign

But whether you walk the journey a little way or continue to learn and walk it a lifetime, you will be helping to save the Cherokee language. Someday you can look back and see the beginning of your journey and see the milestones that mark the progress you have made. Who knows, maybe someday you'll make an entire movie in the Cherokee language or write a book of your own in the Cherokee language or teach someone else and pass on to others what you've learned, whether a little or a lot, to help save the Cherokee language.

ii SSY *vv gadugi*, 'Yes, working together' we can save the GWY SⱰhꙘꙮꙆ *tsalagi gawonihisdi*, 'Cherokee language.'

CHAPTER SIX

Making Friends With Verbs

MARY RAE

Ed once said that when you come across a word you don't know, you should act as if you want to make the word's acquaintance. He said to say '*siyo*' and to invite the word into your home and tell it have a seat and get comfortable. Then get to know the word as if you were making a new friend, and let the word do the talking. If you are patient and listen to what it has to say, you will come to understand it, as you would a friend. That is wonderful advice. Especially when looking at verbs.

Before you read any further, please know that this section on verbs may go into more detail than some students are interested in at this time. If, after reading a paragraph or two, you feel that is the case, please skip this chapter for now. You can always return at a later date.

Cherokee verbs present the greatest challenge to second-language learners. English is an analytic language, which means that it uses words such as prepositions and particles to show how words are related and to get sentence meaning across. Cherokee, on the other hand, is a polysynthetic language, which means that verbs are made up of different morphemes, or meaningful parts. Every Cherokee verb is composed of at least three parts: a pronoun prefix, telling who is doing the action; the stem, which tells what that action is and how it is done; and the tense suffix, which comes towards the end of the word and tells when the action occurs. This is a lot to take in, so Figure 6.1 can help you visualize the basic structure of the verb.

Pronoun Prefix	Verb Stem	Tense Suffix
Who is doing the action	What the action is. It may be Active or Passive	When the action occurs

Figure 6.1. Visualizing the Verb

The face represents the person doing the action. The action can be either active, represented by the wavy lines, or passive, represented by the horizontal lines. The clock represents when the action occurs.

Some linguists may break the verb stem down further into the root, which tells the action of the verb, and a root suffix, sometimes called a theme suffix. The root suffix contains information on how the action takes place: whether the verb's action is ongoing or completed. My descriptions break the verb into three parts, but as you get further along in your studies you can decide which way of looking at the verb is most helpful to you.

In addition, there can be prefixes in front of the pronoun prefix as well as non-final suffixes, and then final suffixes that come after the tense suffix. All of these can alter and refine the meaning of the verb.

When I was first learning, trying to use verbs was like juggling flaming batons. What? Three parts to the verb aren't enough? Here, juggle four, or five or six. I didn't have many successful performances at first. There was so much to keep track of. Still, Cherokee was really captivating. I really wanted to be able to find my way around in the language. Maybe just three batons to start.

Cherokee students may look at the tangle of verbs and think, 'Okay, I just need to get a Cherokee dictionary, and it will all become easy.' Using an English dictionary would help new learners of English find any word they want. Not so in Cherokee.

I am not saying you shouldn't depend upon a dictionary. It is really important to have access to one. But it can be very hard to even find a verb in the dictionary at first. It's usually not that the word isn't there; it just may not be there in the form for which a student is searching. If a brave student were to search the dictionary for the word ᏛᏍᎯᏯᏜ *daganigisi*, she or he would have no luck finding it under words that begin with Ꮃ *da*. That's because the Cherokee dictionary lists words under third person singular present tense, as in, 'he, she or it is walking.' A new student may not yet know that Ꮃ *da-* is a future tense prefix that is attached in front of the pronoun prefix. They probably don't know that Ꮢ *-ga-* contains the pronoun prefix *g-* which indicates first person singular, 'I.' They also may not have learned that the *-i* on the end is a future tense ending.

So, a perfectly well-meaning, highly motivated student may try to look up ᏛᏍᎯᏯᏜ *daganigisi* and end up shredding their notebook after coming up empty-handed. I understand. It should be heartening to know that time and study, along with close attention to introductory material in your dictionary, will help. You will actually be able to find words. Be patient. And just to save you from pulling out your hair, I will share this: ᏛᏍᎯᏯᏜ *daganigisi* means, 'I am going to leave.' You can find the entry for 'he or she is leaving' in the dictionary as ᎠᎯᏯᏗ *a/h/nigia*.

The complicated nature of Cherokee verbs also makes it challenging to begin using the language by creating your own sentences. In English, if you know how to say 'I am going to go to the store,' it's very easy to learn to substitute 'is' when you want to talk about 'he or she,' or 'are' when you want to have a sentence using 'they.' 'Janey *is* going to go to the store,' or 'Janey and her mom *are* going to go to the store.' In Cherokee, there's a little more to it. This is because the information about who is going to the store is added onto the verb stem as a pronoun prefix. In the sentence ᏗᏓᎾᏅ ᏓᎧᏏ *didananv dagesi*, 'I am going to go to the store,' ᏓᎧᏏ *dagesi* tells that I am the one who is going to go. The *g-* in this word is the pronoun prefix that means 'I.' In the sentence Ʋh ᏗᏓᎾᏅ ᏓᏰᏏ *tseni* ('Janey') *didananv* ('the store') *dayesi* ('he or she is going to go'), 'Janey is going to go to the store,' ᏓᏰᏏ *dayesi* tells that she or he is going to go. Lastly, in the sentence Ʋh ᎤᏥᎰᏃ ᏗᏓᎾᏅ ᏛᏁᏏ *tseni* ('Janey') *utsi/h/no* ('and her mother') *didananv* ('the store') *dvnesi* ('they are going to go'), 'Janey and her mother are going to go to the store,' ᏛᏁᏏ *dvnesi* shows that two or more people are going to go. On top of all that, if you look up the word 'store' in the dictionary you will find ᎠᏓᎾᏅ *adananv*. It does mean 'store,' but if you or someone else is going to the store you need to use the prefix *di-* which shows that the store is at a distance from where you are now. So, ᏗᏓᎾᏅ *didananv* is 'store,' but at a distance.

If you wanted to write 'Janey and her mother are going to go to the store,' but construct the English sentence as if it were Cherokee you could have something like this:

Ʋh ᎤᏥᎰᏃ   ᏗᏓᎾᏅ   ᏛᏁᏏ
Janey hermotherand distancestore willbetheygowillbe

You can see how much Cherokee packs into verbs.

Making even simple Cherokee sentences requires quite a lot of juggling. This can be frustrating at first, but if new students remember to go slow and master one thing at a time, they will make their way to the center ring before long and juggle with the best of them. I'd like to help you all learn how.

We've established that Cherokee verbs have a number of moving parts. As we know, the verb is made up of at least three basic parts:

The pronoun prefix, the stem, and the tense suffix. There are also two different categories of verbs: Set A verbs are usually verbs of action, while Set B verbs tend to be more passive or descriptive of a state. The important point here is that Set A and Set B verbs take different sets of pronoun prefixes. Now, wouldn't it be nice if you could learn how to substitute different prefixes and suffixes, to make a lot of different verbs? Actually, you can.

Consider ᎯᏫᏂᎭ *tsiwoniha*, 'I am speaking,' which we saw in Chapter Four. You may recall that *tsi-* is a first person singular pronominal prefix, and shows that I am the one speaking. We can visualize this as before. In this case, the face will represent first person singular, 'I.' (See Figure 6.2).

Pronoun Prefix	Verb Stem	Tense Suffix
Who is doing the action	What the action is. It may be Active or Passive	When the action occurs
tsi	wonih	a

Figure 6.2. Visualizing *tsiwoniha*

If you look at the Set A Pronoun Prefixes chart (Table 6.1), you will be able to substitute other prefixes to show who is involved in the action. For example, if you want to say, 'You are speaking,' look at the column on the left and find 'you,' under 'Second Person.' Moving to the right you will find the Set A prefix for you is *hi-*, so *hiwoniha* means, 'You are speaking.'

You will notice that *hi-* is under a heading which reads, 'Before a consonant.' The prefixes are just a little different before a verb stem that

TABLE 6.1. Set A Pronoun Prefixes

SET A PRONOUN PREFIXES		
	gawoniha he or she is speaking	ega he or she is going
FIRST PERSON	Before a consonant	Before a vowel
I	tsi-/ **tsi**-woniha	g- / **g**-ega
You and I	ini-/ **ini**-woniha	in-/ **in**-ega
All of us and You	idi-/ **idi**-woniha	id- / **id**-ega
Another and I (you are not included)	osdi-/**osdi**-woniha	osd-/ **osd**-ega
They and I (you are not included)	otsi- /**otsi**-woniha	ots- /**ots**-ega
SECOND PERSON	Before a consonant	Before a vowel
You	hi- / **hi**-woniha	h- /**h**-ega
You two	sdi- /**sdi**-woniha	sd- /**sd**-ega
You all, 3 or more	itsi- / **itsi**-woniha	its- /**its**-ega
THIRD PERSON	Before a consonant	Before a vowel
She, he, it	a- or ga- /**ga**-woniha	- /-ega
They	ani- / **ani**-woniha	an- / **an**-ega

Note that the third person before the vowels o-, u- and v-, will use g-. For example: gudalvsga/ he or she is connecting.

begins with a consonant, and before a verb stem that begins with a vowel. If you look at the verb in the next column, you will see *ega*, 'He, she or it is going.' 'Go' is another Set A verb, but the verb stem begins with a vowel, *e-*, so the prefixes are different. If you would like to say, 'They and I are going,' look at 'They and I,' listed under 'First Person,' then slide over to the right to find 'They and I are going,' *otsega*.

Now we can turn to a Set B verb. An example is 'want.' It falls into the Set B category because it refers to a state rather than an action. We will find possible prefixes for this type of verb on the Set B Pronoun Prefixes chart (see Table 6.2). Find the verb in the right-hand column, under 'First Person,' 'I,' *aquaduliha*, 'I want it.' It is under the heading of 'Before a vowel,' because the stem starts with a vowel, *a*.

Table 6.2. Set B Pronoun Prefixes

SET B PRONOUN PREFIXES		
	uha he or she has it	**uduliha** he or she wants it
FIRST PERSON	Before a consonant	Before a vowel
I	agi-/ **agi**-ha	aqu-/ **aqu**-aduliha
You and I	gini-/ **gini**-ha	gin-/ **gin**-aduliha
All of us and You	igi-/ **igi**-ha	ig- / **ig**-aduliha
Another and I (you are not included)	ogini-/**ogini**-ha	ogin-/ **ogin**- aduliha
They and I (you are not included)	ogi- /**ogi**-ha	og- /**og**-aduliha
SECOND PERSON	Before a consonant	Before a vowel
You	tsa- / **tsa**-ha	ts- /**ts**- aduliha
You two	sdi- /**sdi**-ha	sd- /**sd**- aduliha
You all, 3 or more	itsi- / **itsi**-ha	its- /**itsi**- aduliha
THIRD PERSON	Before a consonant	Before a vowel
She, he, it	u- / **u**-ha	uw- (a-)* / **u**-duliha
They	uni- / **uni**-ha	un- / **un**- aduliha

* The third person, she, he it u- before the vowel a is deleted and becomes a-.

Let's imagine that you were at a restaurant with your friend and you both wanted the last piece of frybread. Using the chart, move down the left column until you find 'Another and I,' under 'First Person.' 'We want it,' (the two of us), would be *oginaduliha*. This won't resolve the issue of who gets the frybread, but at least you can state the problem.

You can use the same tactics for *uha*, 'he or she has it,' (a solid thing). You'll notice it is under the 'Before a consonant' heading, because the stem starts with a consonant, *h*-. You might need this chart if a neighbor has a new car and you want to spread the word around the neighborhood. Look down the left column to find, 'She, he, it.' Looking across to the right, you find *uha*. Now you can tell everyone: *ni* ('Look!') *tseni* ('Janey') *itse* ('new') *daqualela* ('car') *uha* ('she has it')— 'Look! Janey has a new car!'

There are additional pronoun prefixes you will come across. Some important ones are used when there is an animate (living) object acted upon by a first or second person. For example, ᏎᏆᎩ *gatvgia*, means, 'I hear it.' The prefix here is *g*-. But if you want to say that you are hearing a person, you would need a different prefix. ᏥᏩᏆᎩ *tsiyatvgia*, 'I hear him or her,' uses the prefix *tsiy*-. The prefix *tsiy*- indicates that I am doing something to someone, not to something. In Figure 6.3 The face on the left represents 'I,' and the face with glasses represents third person singular (he or she). The arrow indicates 'I' to 'you.' The action of the verb is 'hear,' and the tense suffix *a*, represented beneath the clock, shows it is present tense.

Pronoun Prefix	Verb Stem	Tense Suffix
Who is doing the action (to whom)	What the action is. It may be Active or Passive	When the action occurs
tsiy	atvgi	a

Figure 6.3. Visualizing *tsiyatvgia*

For, now, just be aware that you will see those prefixes as your studies progress.

It would be simpler if every verb had only three parts, but as we have already seen, there can also be other prefixes, called 'initial prefixes,' that come before the pronoun prefix. These prefixes will add meaning to the verb, and usually occur in the order in which they are shown below. Table 6.3 shows a chart of the Initial Prefixes as seen in the *Cherokee-English Dictionary*.[1] (Note that prefixes in the same box of this chart cannot be used together).

Table 6.3. Initial Prefixes

1	2	3	4
y- negative ts- relative, past	w- away from speaker	n- lateral position, already	de- plural object
5	6	7	8
da- future da- motion toward speaker di- distant position	i- again	ga- since e- distant imperative	Pronoun Prefixes

Looking at the box, you will see *de-*, for plural object. To see how this would work, consider the phrase, ᎧᏲ ᏣᏍᎵᏆ *quana* ('peach') *tsaduliha* ('you want it'), 'You want a peach.' If you would like to say 'You want peaches,' the word for peach wouldn't change, but you would indicate more than one peach by adding *de-* to the front of the verb: ᎧᏲ ᏍᏣᏍᎵᏆ *quana detsaduliha*, 'You want peaches.'

For another example of initial prefixes, we can look at box 2. We see that *w-* indicates away from speaker. We can understand this by looking at the word ᏧᎢ *ai*, 'he or she is walking.' If we attach the *w-* prefix, *w-* + *ai*, we then have ᏩᎢ *wai*, which says, 'he or she is walking away.'

The verbs discussed here so far have been in the present tense form (sometimes also called *present continuous*). This means that they refer to something that is happening now. It would be nice if the verb stems always stayed the same, but that isn't the case.

There are five different stems, also called *aspect stems*, for each verb, and they are not the same from verb to verb. So you will need to study each verb carefully to understand what the stems are and how they apply. Below you will find a basic description of the five aspect stems:

The Present Aspect Stem is used for actions which are occurring in the present time.

The Immediate Aspect Stem is used for actions that have very recently taken place. It is also used for commands to be acted upon immediately.

The Incompletive Aspect Stem is used in several tenses that show actions that have not yet been completed.

The Completive Aspect Stem is used in several tenses that show actions that have been completed.

The Infinitive Aspect Stem is most often used to express obligation or possibility. You can think of infinitives as "to do it" words. In English, for example 'to sing,' and 'to run,' are infinitives.

This Stem chart (see Table 6.4) shows the different aspect stems for 'speaking.' The stems are the bases upon which different tenses are built. As you can see, several tenses may be formed on one stem. In the left-hand column, you will see the five aspect stems: Present; Immediate; Incompletive; Completive; and Infinitive. Just to the right, you will see the meanings that are possible when you use the stems. Next you will find the pronoun prefixes, the aspect stems, and then, on the far right, the tense endings.

You are already familiar with *tsiwoniha*. If you look at Incompletive Aspect Stem and move to the right, you can choose 'I speak, always,' and see that it is, *tsiwonisgoi*. Using the same stem, you can say, 'I was speaking,' *tsiwonisgvi*, and 'I will be speaking,' *tsiwonisgesdi*.

Using the Set A and Set B Prefixes charts, along with the Stem chart, you will be able to speak, read and write a number of words. Keep in mind that Set B words will almost always use only Set B prefixes, but Set A verbs will *also* use Set B prefixes for the completive past tenses and for the infinitive. By consulting the Set A and Set B Prefixes charts, you can choose the proper prefixes and substitute them into the Stem chart. For example, if you want to say, 'We will be speaking,' choose the Set A prefix for 'all of us and you,' *idi-*. Add it to Incompletive Aspect Stem and with the proper ending for, 'will be speaking,' and you will have *idiwonisgesdi*, 'We all will be speaking.'

Table 6.4. Aspect Stems

	Translation	Pronoun prefix	Stem	Tense suffix
Present Aspect Stem	I am speaking	tsi-	-wonih-	-a
Immediate Aspect Stem	Speak! You just spoke	hi- hi-	-wonih- -wonih-	-i -a
Incompletive Aspect Stem	I speak, always I was speaking I will be speaking	tsi- tsi- tsi-	-wonisg- -wonisg- -wonisg-	-oʔi -vʔi -esdi
Completive Aspect Stem	I spoke You spoke (reportedly) You speak! (Later) I will speak	agi- tsa- hi- da-tsi-	-wonis- -wonis- -wonis- -wonis-	-vʔi -eʔi -vʔi -i
Infinitive Aspect Stem	He or she to speak He or she has to speak	u- u-	-wonihis- -wonihis-	-di -di

In Table 6.4, you will notice tense suffixes in the right-hand column. To more clearly understand their use, review the following verb tense endings:

-a, -i present (it is happening now)
   recent past (it happened just now or recently)
   imperative (command)
-oʔi habitual (it always is, it usually is)
-vʔi remote past (it happened in the past)
   future imperative, (a command, but to be done at a future time)
-eʔi reportative past, (it happened in the past, but you weren't
   there to witness it)
-esdi future progressive (it will be happening)
-i future (when combined with *da-* or *dv-* before the pronoun
   prefix, it will happen)
-di infinitive (to do it)

This information goes a long way towards helping you understand verbs you come across. You can look for pronoun prefixes,
remembering that they may not be at the very front. You can look
for any familiar verb stem to get an idea what the verb is talking
about. Then you can find possibilities for when the action of the
verb takes place by looking for tense endings.

It sounds as if everything is all neatly wrapped up. Only, it isn't.
Yes, there are still more batons to juggle.

There are other non-final suffixes that may attach to the verb
stem to slightly alter the meaning of the verb. For example, ᎤᏬᏂᏒᎢ
uwonisvi means 'he or she spoke.' But when we attach the completive suffix, *-ohn-*, to the completive verb stem, we have ᎤᏬᏂᏐᏅᎢ,
uwonisohnvi, 'he or she finished speaking.'

A number of final suffixes can also add meaning to words, and
not just verbs. One final suffix, Ꮹ *-quu*, adds the meaning of 'just,'
or 'only.' For example, ᎠᏯᏩ *ayaquu*, means 'just me.'

There are also several question suffixes: *-s* added to the end of a
word makes a word a question. ᏒᎦᏔ *svg(a)ta*, for example, is 'apple,'
but ᏒᎦᏔᏍ *svg(a)tas*, would ask, 'An apple?' or 'Is it an apple?'
When the question suffix *-ke* is attached to a word that is paired

with a word ending in *-s*, it has the meaning of 'or.' For example, DTᎣ DCᏂ *ais atlike*, 'Is she walking or is she running?' Another question suffix, *-tsu* is similar to *-s*, but adds the additional meaning of asking about something that was expected to happen. DSᎣSᏍ *agasgatsu*, might be translated as, 'It's raining, isn't it?' or 'So, is it raining?' The suffix Ꮎ *-na* adds the meaning of 'What about?' For example, DᎩᏜᏂᎾ *agilisina*, asks, 'What about my grandmother?'

Having looked at the basic components of the Cherokee verb, it is now easy to break down even rather long words like, ᎤᏂᏤᏙᎵᏆᎣ *widagedoliquu*, 'I am just going to go over there.' (See Table 6.5).

Table 6.5. *Widagedoliquu*

Initial Prefix	Pronoun Prefix	Stem	Non-final Suffix	Tense Suffix	Final Suffix
wi- (away) + **da-** (future)	**g-** (I)	**-edol-** (to be here), completive stem		**-i-** (future)	**-quu** (just, only)

Notice that every part of the verb follows a specific order. For example, *wi-* comes before *da-*, as was seen in the Initial Prefixes chart, Table 6.3.

There are a number of rules to learn that will change the prefixes slightly. For example, if you want to say, 'You are just going to go over there,' you would use the *h-* personal pronoun for 'you.' But when *h-* is preceded by *da-* for future, they combine and become *-t-*. So, the resulting word would be ᎤᏸᏤᏙᎵᏆᎣ *witedoliquu*, 'You are just going to go over there.'

You will pick up the rules as you go along. As long as you have a basic idea of the structure of the verb, you will be able to fit everything into place. Just not all at once. Here again, patience will be your best friend.

This is a simplified glance at verbs and how they work, but it should help lay the groundwork for more in-depth study. It's important for learners to have some idea how the language works. Most students, even those who were intimidated at first by the complexity of Cherokee verbs, find themselves marveling at how parts of the language fit together like clockwork. Grammar helps us to understand the inner workings.

We should all remember, however, that focusing entirely on grammar takes the student outside of the language, away from speaking and from reading and writing. Here, I confess my secret about Cherokee grammar. I would like to learn as much as I can, then forget it. Entirely. I would like to speak, read and write Cherokee without ever thinking about pronominal prefixes or non-experienced past suffixes. I would like to dissolve the entire framework of the grammatical structure of Cherokee, and just see Cherokee as a part of life, from inside the language.

That is my dream. That is what I strive for everyday. But, as a member of the community of language learners and teachers, I also feel a responsibility to learn as much as I can about all aspects of the language so that I can help others learn. My hope is that they, in turn, will contribute by using the language, perhaps translating and analyzing old documents, helping to preserve them for future generations. Maybe they will write down their own stories in Cherokee syllabary that people one-hundred years from now will read.

Make friends with verbs. You don't make good friends overnight, so don't try to take in everything about the verbs all at once. Take your time making their acquaintance. Try to recall what you've read. Go back and review. Look into other sources to see what they say. Familiarize yourself with the basic structure of verbs then look more deeply into the details as you go along. It is an amazing feeling when you can fit all the pieces together. Being able to understand a verb, even a simple one, is an accomplishment to be celebrated. And there is always more to learn, more fascinating details to capture your imagination. Even more batons to juggle.

CHAPTER SEVEN

Which Meaning?

ED FIELDS

ᏏᏲ ᏍᏆᎵᎦ Ꮝ ᏥᏦᏎᏙ *siyo galieliga si tsitsedoa*, 'Hello, I'm glad you all are still here.' By now you probably know that the English and Cherokee worldviews are different and these differences make the languages differ. If we were in class I could do various things to try to help you get the meanings for Cherokee words, phrases and sentences.

In the Cherokee online class you can see the slides with the lessons on them, and I can underline things or point things out and explain things. I can draw pictures to illustrate words or meanings. I can pronounce words and re-pronounce or explain meanings and interact with you in the chat by answering questions or talking about things. So that, even if you didn't understand many words in Cherokee, you'd be able to see the writings on my part.

And I could tell you what the prefix is and the root is and what the suffix is saying—the front and the middle and the end of the word (the prefix tells who is involved and how many; the plural maker is also in the prefix, that tells you who and how many; the root tells you what the verb is; the suffix tells you the tense, whether it's present, past, future and so on). And you could ask questions like 'why does this word have that and the other doesn't' and such, and I could explain it to you.

I could even tell you some original word meanings. For example, ᏏᏍᏩ *svg(a)ta* the part of that word *gata* is 'it is hanging'—an apple hangs from a tree. ᏏᏍᏩ *svg(a)ta* hangs from a tree. Another example, is the color red, the red is ᎩᎦᎨ *gigage* and the part that says *giga* refers to the blood. So that maybe is where the ancestors got the word for the red color, from the color of blood.

Of course, we're not in class, and a chapter is limited by pages, but I will try to draw some pictures to illustrate for you one word that contains two sentences, so you can see meaning. And I will try to draw some pictures to illustrate a key point I call Finding the 'X' or Looking at the 'X,' as it may help you in your journey. And I will talk a little about meanings and a little about translating. I hope this helps you.

Cherokee and English are like apple and peach. Both are fruits, but apple is not peach and peach is not apple. English and Cherokee are both languages, but English is not Cherokee and Cherokee is not English. For one thing, Cherokee is descriptive. The words are describing something to you. They are drawing, painting, making or forming a picture for you.

You get to know the Cherokee verb by listening to what it says. It's telling you something, it's describing something to you. Kind of like someone talking to you, describing something to you. For instance, someone says ᎠᎾᏬ ᏕᏍᎩᏅᏥ *ahnawo desginvsi*. The word *desginvsi* is describing a flexible item, it is describing what *ahnawo* is. So, *desginvsi* is saying 'give me something that is in flexible form.' For example, a shirt, it's not hard, it's not long and slender, and it's not living. That one word is like 'you give me the flexible item,' so that's kind of like what it says to you, is telling you.

ahnawo desginvsi, 'give me something flexible' [*ahnawo* 'shirt'] *usdi desgikasi,* 'give me something living' [*usdi* 'baby' (pronounced with elongated *u—uusdi)*]

ama desginehvsi, 'give me something liquid' [*ama* 'water']

digowelodi desgidisi 'give me something elongated/slender and rigid' [*digowelodi,* 'pencil']

asquatlesdi deskvsi 'give me something neutral' [*asquatlesdi* 'ball'] Remember, what doesn't fit in the other categories fits in the neutral category.

As you can see, the English verb differs from the Cherokee verb because the Cherokee verb includes more information, it tells you more, it's descriptive. If you were speaking, reading, writing or translating Cherokee, then the English verb and the Cherokee verb would not be able to be matched exactly. You would look at the English verb and ask who is asking to be given something, and what are they asking to be given. And then you'd need more words added to your sentence in English. In Cherokee, one verb can do it.

Let's look at another word. ᎣᎵᎥᏙᎵ *widagedoli.* (See Figure 7.1).

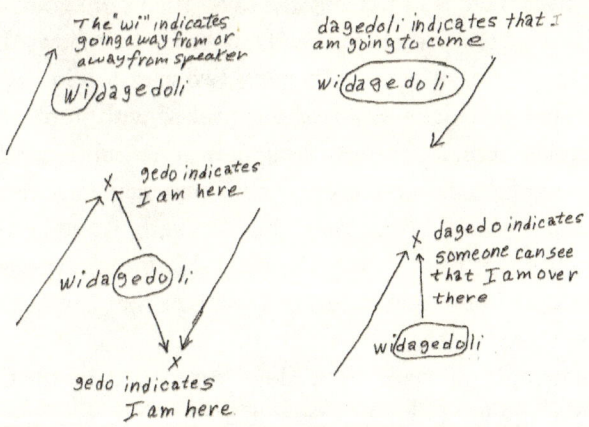

Figure 7.1. Widagedoli

The *wi* says 'away from here' or some say going away from a speaker, from the person doing the speaking. It indicates the person is going away from here to elsewhere, to somewhere, a place. The arrow is pointing away from the starting point, away from the speaker, the starting point or the speaker is located at the blunt end of the arrow.

And the *dagedoli* says 'I am going to come' but it shows 'I'm going to come back.' So the arrow is now pointing back towards the starting point, back to where the speaker is located.

So that's to and fro. Going and coming back here. So that's what it means. 'I'm going to come.'

Now let's look at *gedo*. Notice the arrows showing going to and fro. One pointing away, and one returning, the two we just talked about. The smaller middle arrows there pointing in two directions, the two arrows starting from the word *gedo*, indicate where I am at. Wherever I am at, if I'm over there somewhere, at the first X (away from speaker), then *gedo*, 'I am here.' Or, when I come back, at the second X (returning to the speaker), then *gedo*, 'I am here.'

And the *dagedo* says 'I am over there.' So it's like picturing me over there away from here, *dagedo*.

If you make a sentence with *widagedoli*, it goes like this 'I am going over there' and the *dagedoli* says 'Then I am going to come' (and since I 'come back here' then I am 'here'), so it shows 'Then I am going to come back here.' So there are two sentences in *widagedoli*—compound sentence—*widagedoli* is packed with information. It's a Cherokee verb, it has everything in it. It has subject, verb, direct object—in fact, in two places, as both sentences have them.

All those words are in one Cherokee verb. As you can see this differs from an English verb. In English, all those words are in a sentence, or in two sentences. In Cherokee they can be contained in one "word," in the verb.

Remember, all you need to do is to get to know the Cherokee verb like you get to know a person, spend time listening to them and letting them tell you about some things. The more you listen, the more you let them talk, the more you know about them, the more you know them. They have a lot to say, a lot to tell you, a lot of information for you.

When you're getting to know a Cherokee verb, you'll see it has a lot of information-giving words like verb, subject, direct object, etc., packed into it. You have to 'unpack' them. Like conversations with people, you have to have patience, you know there is a way to go about getting to know a person, it is usually a little at a time, until over time you know them well enough you can pick out their voice in a room crowded with other peoples' voices.

Now let's look at a key point I call Finding the 'X' or Looking at the 'X.'

In Chapter One I told you that English has around forty definitions for the word 'bear' while in Cherokee to say 'bear' you'd say ᏘᎾ *yona*. But did you know that ᏘᎾ *yona* does not really mean 'bear?' 'Bear' is not a Cherokee word. ᏘᎾ *yona* is a Cherokee word. So how do you think people began to say that ᏘᎾ *yona* meant 'bear'?

Think back in time, long ago, to when English speakers and Cherokee speakers first met. Let's say the Cherokee speakers were here—see 'C' below—and the English speakers were here—see 'E' below. (See Figure 7.2).

Comprehension
Both know what the X is
Both know which animal it is

English words don't mean cheroki
words and vice versa even when
talking about same thing
They use their own words

Figure 7.2. Finding the X

The Cherokee speakers couldn't understand the English speakers. And the English speakers couldn't understand the Cherokee speakers. Let's say one of the English speakers spoke something. But the Cherokee speakers could not understand.

But when the English speaker showed or pointed at what it was, the 'X,' then the Cherokee speakers could see what they were talking about, they were talking about the 'X.' Otherwise they would not have known.

And so they, the English speakers, have their words. And the Cherokee speakers have their words. So that's what they'll say. But it doesn't really mean English words mean Cherokee words, and vice versa. They are talking about the same thing, but each is using their words, their worldviews.

So both have to have this pointing at the 'X' to know what they each are talking about. Then those who see the speaker pointing at the 'X' and hear the speaker's words, even if they don't know the other language, will know what the speaker means.

So, a long time ago, one of them would have pointed at something and pronounced it in their language. Let's say, one of them pointed at a large four-legged animal, that was furry and growled. They thought and said 'bear.' But the Cherokee, looking at that same animal, thought and said *yona*. They were both looking at the 'X,' a common object or thing, and both naming it in their language. They were beginning to communicate, to learn what words each other called things and thought about things.

Maybe they pointed at water, said 'water' and did the motion for 'drink.' And the Cherokee understood the English person wanted *ama* to drink. Maybe they did these things a lot, pointing at the 'X' and making motions. They basically painted a picture. They could have looked at the 'X' and understood. Then they could each do this again and again, pointing at another 'X' and coming to learn to communicate.

The 'X' is something that is talked about or that can be seen. Let's say a Cherokee speaker is talking about something, but the

English speaker does not know that language. In order for either of them to know what the other is talking about, they have to say the words and point at 'X'.

English has been around for a long time now, but there are still Cherokee elders who may not know what the English speaker is saying. So finding 'X' can help you communicate better with them.

You find something that you both know, although each in your different languages, and use it as a point of reference. These days sometimes you still have to see the 'X' to know. Like when someone wants to translate for you, or you translate for somebody. They might not see what you're talking about, until you show them the 'X.'

Finding the 'X' helps you understand each other, helps you understand what the person, who does not speak your language, is referring to.

Now I will talk a little about meanings and translating.

A word in the English language can have a lot of meanings. When you are interacting in the two languages, you need to find out which meaning is meant. This is especially important when you are translating. And, sooner or later, someone is going to ask you to translate. Or you may want to translate something for yourself. That may even be why you came to class. At any rate, as you proceed on your journey into the Cherokee language, you'll eventually reach the need to translate for yourself or for someone else.

When you do, remember that you need to find out which meaning is meant by the text or called for in the text or wanted by the person asking for the translation. If you don't find out the specific meaning they want, then they won't be satisfied when you give them the translation and you will find that it is taking a lot of your time too.

Many years ago, around two decades now, someone asked me to translate something in English into Cherokee for them. So I worked at it until I got the meaning as close as I could get it, but when I told them, they did not like the meaning, they said that was not what they wanted. They then repeated their request and

I translated it again, but with a different meaning. Again, they didn't like it. So I translated it again and I finally got the meaning they wanted.

This taught me to ask ahead of time which specific meaning the person is asking for in English. English words have more than one meaning. You, the translator, need to know which meaning is wanted. Does the person wanting the translation mean 'bear' as in the animal, or 'bear' as in carry, or 'bear' as in endure, and so on. So when you are asked to translate something, always narrow the requested meaning down as specifically as the person is able to tell you. This will help you both.

Knowing the meanings of words is especially important when you translate. You can't just hunt through a word list and find "matches."

For instance, let's say Jimmy's friend just got a new puppy. She says all the puppy seems to want to do is zip around the house yipping, so she is going to name the puppy 'zip-and-yip.' She wants Jimmy to translate the phrase into Cherokee. Jimmy is feeling confident, he already knows one of the three words—he knows 'and' in Cherokee is DᎤ *ale*—so the translation is one-third done already. He says it's just a matter of finding two more words—'zip' and 'yip.' Jimmy searches through word lists and dictionaries and online sites (not knowing that some dictionaries and online sites are basically word lists too, even though they may have a brief definition sometime), and he finds the word 'zip.' He writes it down ᎭᎦᏁᎦ *hikanega*, 'zip.' Then he searches for 'yip,' but can't find it. So he figures 'yelp' will do, but can't find it. Then he thinks that since 'yip' and 'yelp' are the same as 'bark,' that he'll search for 'bark.' He finds 'bark.' He writes it down ᎤᏯᎸ *uyalv* 'bark.' And then Jimmy puts all the words together for his friend. He shows her the translation, he tells her the translation and he helps her learn how to pronounce *hikanega ale uyalv*. She goes around telling everyone she knows and meets the Cherokee name for her puppy, and when they ask her what it means in English, she says it means 'zip-and-yip.'

But does it really mean that?

No.

Let's say another of Jimmie's friends has found some old diaries from her aunt. She never met her aunt because her aunt died long before she was born, but she feels really drawn to this aunt through reading the diaries. Her aunt's favorite expressions were 'I got the heebie-jeebies' and 'that gave me the heebie-jeebies.' Jimmie's friend wants to name her car 'heebie-jeebies,' but she wants it translated into Cherokee. Which of the following do you think Jimmie should do?

1. Tell her since the words already have Cherokee sounds, she can use the Cherokee sounds: hee = hi, and gee = tsi and s = s. And since the ending 'ie' is basically equal to 'i', she can use 'i'. So she really only needs to find a Cherokee substitute for 'b,' so just pick a consonant like 'l' or 'w' to substitute for it, then the word can be spelled with Cherokee characters like this: heebie-jeebies = hili-tsilis.

2. Tell her to look up and use the Cherokee word for the English word 'he,' the English word 'jee' or 'gee' and for 'be.' And instead of having 'ie' at the end, put the Cherokee 'i.' And use the Cherokee 's.'

3. Tell her to look the entire word up in a dictionary that will include terms used during the time her aunt wrote the diaries in the 1930s. Read through each meaning listed under the word, and match the meaning with the contextual meaning that is meant in her aunt's diaries. Then use that meaning to search for a similar meaning in Cherokee.

Let's say your relative bought a used truck in great shape, he calls it his 'Trusty Bucket of Bolts' and wants to name it that in Cherokee. How do you go about translating it in Cherokee? Do you go by the whole meaning, or each word's meaning or a little of both?

Or let's say you find a page from a little notebook that is a list your great grandmother wrote. The little list contains a dozen family members' names. Ten names are written in English and, at the bottom of the list, two names are written in Cherokee syllabary. But time and many moves to different homes and locations have not been kind to the little list. Over time, a small triangular piece of it was torn out of the page. It leaves the bottom of the page that lists the two names in Cherokee syllabary with only some of the syllabary characters intact, while a few are missing. But how many characters are missing? And what were the names? How can you find out?

Your teenage daughter has a school assignment to pick a brief English saying and translate it into Cherokee. She stays overnight at her aunt and uncle's home and watches a movie with her uncle where a woman, who happens to be a daughter too, yells 'Down with all tyrants!' Your daughter thinks that is a great English saying to use to translate into Cherokee. You want to help her, so how do you go about it?

Think about it, how would you go about translating 'longshoreman'—is it a man who is as long as a sea's shore, or something else? How about 'twinkle-toes'—is it a person who has toes that twinkle, or is it something else? And does the person wanting the translation use the English words for what the English dictionary says they mean, or does that person have their own meaning for the words?

These and other adventures happen to Cherokee translators almost daily, and even to students who are learning the Cherokee language. People tend to think it's easy to translate from English into Cherokee, and vice versa. They don't realize the two worldviews require a little bit of effort, and sometimes it can be a challenge to get to a meaning that is close.

Meanings are important things to learn, and you can't just learn them from word lists and sometimes even dictionaries. For one thing, not all Cherokee words are in the lists and dictionaries. Not all Cherokee words are even in the Cherokee Bible and old books and documents. For another thing, a word list and even some dictionaries can't give you 'common knowledge.' A first-language Cherokee speaker can look through a word list or a dictionary and when they find a word they can look at the definition, if it has one, and know if it's the right meaning. Or if it doesn't have a definition, they can know if that word means the meaning they need and want, as they have 'common knowledge' that has been imparted to them. While a student is tending to rely only on the definition of the word, and many times that definition is only one word or a few words long.

A second-language learner, who did not research more into the meaning, may take a word and use it to mean what it does not mean, then they will have a translation that does not really say what they think it says (such as Jimmy above, who used zip—to button up a button or zip up a zipper—for zip around the house and bark of a tree for bark of a dog). There are different meanings. You have to get the right one.

So, always research.

Learn the Cherokee meanings and use them as they really were meant to be used. At the same time, do not tie yourselves in knots so much that you are afraid to do anything. Have a balance about it and learn smart.

How do you learn smart when it comes to words and meanings?

Look at the word lists and the dictionary entries and the definitions given if they have any, but then research to see how the word or words were used in context in a written document or letter or publication such as the Cherokee Bible and other Cherokee resources. You may not always be able to find what you're looking for, as not all words are in published resources even today, but there are thousands and thousands that are. So that will help you.

Sometimes with translating, you have something you want translated or someone brings you something to be translated and it is not typed or printing-press printed, instead it is handwritten. Translating handwritten Cherokee is similar to translating typed or printing-press Cherokee syllabary or phonetics, but it differs too. Handwritten Cherokee can call for its own set of tips.

One tip is to compare handwritten Cherokee characters by looking at more than just the one word or one sentence that you have or that was given to you. The person wanting the translation may have only given you one word or one sentence to translate, and you may be tempted to not look at the other words or sentences in the handwritten letter or document, but look at as much of the handwritten letter or document as you need to, or can or are allowed to look at. If they have not provided them, then ask for more. If they provide them, then you'll have more help in translating because you'll have more handwritten characters to compare. If they don't, then you'll have to do the best you can.

At any rate, read as much of the handwritten Cherokee words and sentences as you need to or as you can. Then translate the handwritten word, words, phrases, sentences, paragraphs that you need to or can translate. And then compare what you now have and know to what you don't have and know. The handwritten word and/or sentence that you could not read, you may be able to figure it out by the context that you now have.

The writer of the handwritten Cherokee letter or document will have written each Cherokee character in their own unique style of handwriting. That style will give you enough to go on for you to be able to tell each character from another that may look similar.

For instance, at first glance you may think that the writer is writing a certain character, but when you compare it with what you've read and already translated and/or the context, you realize it is actually a different character. Some words that used the character will be known to you or found in a dictionary or other Cherokee resource, and you'll be able to determine what the character is. Sort of like in English if you had someone's handwritten printed or cursive letter and their m's and n's weren't quite clear, but then you come across words of theirs that definitely would use 'm' instead of 'n.' You see words like 'me, more, money' and you know the writer would not use words like 'ne, nore, nomey,' so you know the instances where the unclear 'm/n' is being used that the character is really an 'm.'

You can do this with each handwritten Cherokee character in the letter or document that you need to do it with. The handwritten character will be used in some Cherokee words and contexts, but not in others. And that will help you figure out what word and what character the writer is using.

Another tip is to use your computer, or other technology, to enlarge the text of the handwritten letter or document. When the text is enlarged, it is easier to see what is a curve or a loop or a gap, etc., and be able to figure out the handwritten Cherokee characters.

Another tip, if you have to translate a very long handwritten letter or document, is to create a comparison list. This is just a list of characters the person hand-wrote in the letter or document. Each time you come across a character, write it in your list the way the writer wrote it, and next to it write a legible version of it.

You can then quickly compare other characters that you come across. This way you don't have to try to remember what each handwritten character looked like, which can be a problem if you are translating very long handwritten letters or documents. It can also be a problem if you are working on two or more different writers' letters or documents during the same day or week, as each will have their own writer's unique style of handwriting. And it can be a problem if you have many pages to search through to find the times the character was used, sometimes a character may have only been used once and you have to find that one time.

You may not have to include all characters made by the writer. You may just have to do it for the ones that are hard for you to decipher. Making a comparison list can take time in the beginning to do, but it can save you time as you go along if the letter or document is very long.

Another thing you'll come across when translating is the usage of *tsa, tse, tsi, tso, tsu, tsv* instead of *ja, je, ji, jo, ju, jv.* Our ancestors used *tsa, tse, tsi, tso, tsu, tsv*. You can see them used in *A Cherokee Spelling Book* by D. S. Butrick and D. Brown, 1819 (which pre-dates the Syllabary). And in *The Cherokee Messenger*, August 1844, the Cherokee language lesson sounds used *tsa, tse, tsi, tso, tsu, tsv*. *The Cherokee Pictorial Book*, 1888, also used them. When I write and when I translate, I prefer to use *tsa, tse, tsi, tso, tsu, tsv* to honor my ancestors.

Second-language learners are capable of learning to hear, pronounce, read, write and translate *tsa, tse, tsi, tso, tsu, tsv*. I've seen second-language learners do it. Just take some time to listen to a first-language speaker pronounce *tsa, tse, tsi, tso, tsu, tsv*, and practice it. You'll get it. And when you run across *tsa, tse, tsi, tso, tsu, tsv* in old documents to translate, you won't be doing mental gymnastics to mentally change 'ts' into 'j' so that you can understand the 'ts' words before you can begin to translate the 'ts' words, you'll be able to jump right in and get to work translating the *tsa, tse, tsi, tso, tsu, tsv* words.

And, as I said, the ancestors pronounced and wrote the words with Ꮳ *tsa*, Ꮴ *tse*, Ꮵ *tsi*, Ꮶ *tso*, Ꮷ *tsu*, Ꮸ *tsv*. You may want to honor them and do the same. I know you are capable of it. Don't sell yourself short. Just give yourself time, and practice. You'll get there.

In previous chapters, I said that it is good to have a home library of Cherokee resources that you can use to learn Cherokee, these resources come in handy when you translate too. When you are translating, check the Cherokee Bible and other Cherokee resources to see if you are getting the Cherokee meaning down.

Sometimes some people shy away from using the Cherokee Bible for various reasons. Maybe like I used to be, they would rather watch movies or something. My parents used to always tell me ᎯᏏ ᎠᎢᏬᏗ ᏏᏲ ᎤᏁᏛᎢᏲᎠ ᏍᏩᏬᎵᏲᏗ *nigav gohusdi gesv Unetlanvhi detsalasgesdi*, 'in all things have yourself placed in Creator, God.' But it took me a while to realize I could read the Bible and still have time to watch movies, and life improved when I started reading it. Also, when it came to the Cherokee language, I found some neato words and meanings in the Cherokee Bible. A Bible translated into a native language makes a great language resource, and it can help save a native language.

Many years ago, I was at a conference on native language survival. A lady told about how her native language had died out and she had wanted to revive it. But there were no speakers left. There was not anything written in her language that she could find. She searched and she searched, she looked so hard, tried so hard, and finally in the Smithsonian she found a Bible that had been translated into her native language. She went through that Bible and she wrote down each word. She used the context contained in that Bible to tell her the meanings of words. And she made a dictionary of thousands and thousands of words in her native language for her people. Her people began to use it to revive their native language.

Anyway, the Cherokee Bible contains thousands and thousands of words, this is why the Cherokee Bible is a good reference resource. You can use the Cherokee Bible along with an English Bible to find words, or you can use *The Cherokee Old Testament (In Part) & Parallel Cherokee & English* along with *The Cherokee New Testament Parallel Cherokee & English* to find words. All those thousands and thousands of words are used in context in the Cherokee Bible, context is good for helping you know or figure out the correct word meanings.

But since there are those thousands and thousands of words, having a good Bible concordance to look up words makes it easier and faster to find the verses in the Bible where the word you want is found. I have not found a Cherokee Bible concordance. But there are ones for the English Bible. You can use one of those concordances to find words in English and where they are located in the English Bible (what Bible books, chapters, verses), and then use that information to locate and look up the words in the Cherokee Bible (what Bible books, chapters, verses). Unfortunately the Cherokee Bible was never completed. It still does not have some books translated. I don't know why.

Another helpful resource is an English dictionary that has word meanings from slightly before the old Cherokee resources were done in the 1800's. Some English words and their meanings changed over the years. You'll want the 1800s' meanings of the English words, phrases and sentences. The translators would have used those meanings to translate the English meanings into Cherokee meanings. So if you use a modern English dictionary it may give you the modern meanings, which are the wrong meanings, and that means you'd end up translating it wrong too.

Besides the Cherokee Bible, you can also find words in other Cherokee resources, such as *Bob the Sailor Boy*, *Poor Sarah* and *The Cherokee Messenger*. *The Cherokee Messenger* also printed *Pilgrim's Progress* by John Bunyan in Cherokee, as well as some of *Peter Parley's Universal History* in Cherokee. This means that you can look at the English versions of *Pilgrim's Progress* and *Peter Parley's Universal History* and compare them with the Cherokee translations of them in the newspaper. You can find Cherokee words and how they were used in context.

It's good to have these resources as physical books or saved as PDFs on your computer or USB device. That way, if the Internet is down or you can't get to the Internet, or individual websites go down or cease to exist, you'll still have your physical and/or saved PDF resources. So having your own library of physical and PDF resources is best. And hunting for Cherokee resources is like hunting for treasure. It's a lot of fun.

I have talked about some translation tips, and hope they help you. Translating can be a lot of fun. I know when Meli and I do a translation session it's usually a really fun, relaxed, interesting and learning time. Translating challenges us to really think sometimes. We have our Cherokee resources handy and use all the Cherokee resources we need, looking up words and their meanings.

Rita, my wife, who has seen Meli and me translating over the phone, says, 'Watching you two translate is like watching two people using everything they have and everything they can get their hands on, including the kitchen sink! You're looking in the Cherokee Bible, looking in dictionaries, looking in the Cherokee newspaper or *Poor Sarah* or Bunyan or getting up to find some other resources on your shelf. You're looking on USBs and searching through notes and papers. Tossing possibilities back and forth to each other. There's a lot going on! It's a lot of fun to watch. Someone ought to make a Cherokee translating show!'

When translating, Meli and I do use every resource we need that we can get our hands on. But another thing we use is what I call 'common knowledge.'

Common knowledge is what speakers and elders have deposited into me. It is what is deposited in your brain, in your mind, in your heart and into you by your teachers. This is why it is important that instructors and teachers of Cherokee deposit all they can into second-language learners. It is also why it is important that learners try to make sure they are getting real knowledge, real meanings. Each elder and speaker is a knowledge keeper or a language treasury—however you want to think of it—and they have this storehouse or treasure of meanings and knowledge of the language and worldview in them. Whatever amount of their storehouse or treasure that is not passed on is the amount of the language and worldview that will be lost.

Someday, should the first-language speakers all be gone, then the second-language learners will be the knowledge keepers or the language treasuries for the Cherokee nation, the Cherokee people—for the world really. And whatever was deposited into the learners by their instructors and teachers, whatever they have learned and whatever they hold on to and keep in them, that will be what is passed on to the ones coming after them. Whatever is lost will be at risk of being lost forever.

It is more important than I can say to pass on the knowledge and language to learners, and for learners to receive it and pass it on to others. It is a circle that has endured, and hopefully that will continue to endure. And hopefully that will thrive and grow. GV *wado*, 'Thank you.'

CHAPTER EIGHT

From One Language to Another

MARY RAE

Translation from one language to another cannot be exact. Every language has its own way of organizing information, and transferring that to another language can only be approximate, at best. A student's life would be so much easier if there were a one-to-one correspondence between English and Cherokee words, but the reality is not quite so simple. I can remember being a fairly new student of Ed's and writing to ask him to translate a phrase into Cherokee. He wrote back asking what exactly did I mean in the original sentence. I was puzzled. Hadn't I told him in my email? After all, he was a native speaker, and I was counting on him to give me an instant answer. Seemed reasonable at the time. What I didn't understand was that because he was a native speaker and a teacher, he knew there was a lot to consider. There could be a number of meanings to the English words themselves, and it was important to establish which meanings I wanted before any translation was begun.

In order to translate from Cherokee to English or from English to Cherokee, the differences between the two languages must be understood. Both English and Cherokee words can often be used in various ways. In English, for example, the verb 'turning' can be used for 'turning it,' 'turning on the light,' 'turning back,' 'turning off the road' and 'turning it over.' All of those sentences use the same verb, 'turning.' In Cherokee, on the other hand, each of those examples would require a completely different verb. Look at the following list of words:

SSꭲꭳꭻꭲ *gadey(a)sdiha*, 'he or she is turning it'
DCꭶꭰꭼꭰꭱ *atsvstvsga*, 'he or she is turning on a light'
DꭵWꭹꭰ *ak(a)tahva*, 'he or she is turning back'
DꭶD *adlea*, 'he or she is turning off the road'
SꭲꮅꭲSS *dekaliquadega*, 'he or she is turning it over'

Each Cherokee verb contains all the information needed to know which type of 'turning' is being referred to.

Similarly, the English word 'running,' applies to many different situations. You can say, 'he or she is running,' 'he or she is taking off running,' 'he or she is running away,' and 'he or she is running for office,' just to name a few. The word 'running,' stays the same, but the words around it change the meaning. In Cherokee, there are four distinct verbs that would be used:

DC *atli*, 'he or she is running'
DꮅꭱGꭲꭻꭲ *adanaw(a)sdiha*, 'he or she is taking off running'
DꮅꭲD *alitia*, 'he or she is running away'
DVꭹꭲD *atogiyaa*, 'he or she is running for office'

In Cherokee, there is no need for additional words to make the meaning clear.

A student might come across the word, Sꭲꮎꭰꮃꭲ *gadanvteha*, 'I am thinking,' and may be tempted to apply that to other meanings of 'think,' such as in the phrase, 'I think so.' In Cherokee, however, there is a completely different verb that would be used. ꭾꮅD *gelia*, 'I think so,' is usually a response and shows an affirmative answer.

Another example of the differences in meaning between English and Cherokee would be the word, 'beginning.' In English, you could say, 'the show is beginning,' or 'she is beginning to study,' and the verb stays the same. In Cherokee, no such luck. DᏝᏍᎭᎠ *adaleniha* is used for 'it is beginning,' while DᏍᎭᎠ *aleniha* would mean, 'he or she is beginning.' To complicate things even further, a student might look up 'start' and find DᎯᎩD *a/h/nigia*, 'it is starting,' which could apply to a car starting, but which can also mean 'he or she is leaving.'

Cherokee has even more to throw at the unsuspecting learner, who only wants to translate a measly word or two about finding something. He or she must first consider whether or not the word he or she wants to use is a classificatory verb. Classificatory verbs are a set of verbs that make distinctions based on five categories: living, liquid, long and rigid, flexible, and neutral. They are very often verbs that have to do with handling something, such as 'have,' 'hold,' 'bring,' 'get,' 'take' and 'find.' Considering the last word, in English you can find a person, a diamond, water, a stick, or a string, and the verb will remain the same. In Cherokee, you need a different form of the verb, depending on which catergory the found object (or being) belongs to. Look at the examples given below for 'finding':

DGᎫᎠ *a/h/watiha*, 'he or she is finding it,' or 'he or she is finding a living thing.'
SᎡGᎫᎠ *gane/h/watiha*, 'he or she is finding liquid.'
DBGᎫᎠ *ayv/h/watiha*, 'he or she is finding something long and rigid.'
SᎧGᎫᎠ *ganaw(a)tiha*, 'he or she is finding something flexible.'

If a student wants to say, 'She found a shirt,' he or she has to first decide which form of 'find' fits. In this case, it would be flexible, since a cloth shirt fits the category. The student would then look up the verb, and figure out the third person (he, she or it) form.

Next, the student would have to decide how to make it past tense: ᎤᏩᏒᎦᎳᏫ *unaw(a)tvhvi,* 'He or she found it.' The word for shirt is *ahnawo,* so ᎠᎤᏩ ᎤᏩᏒᎦᎳᏫ *ahnawo unaw(a)tvhvi* means, 'He or she found a shirt.' Classificatory verbs are very specific, and they picture what is happening. Even if you only saw the word ᎤᏩᏒᎦᎳᏫ *unaw(a)tvhvi,* 'He or she found it,' you would see a picture in your mind of someone who found something flexible, even though you wouldn't know exactly what it was. It might be a piece of cloth, a shirt or a dress, a ribbon, or a piece of paper. You also know that 'he or she' found it, and that it happened in the past. All in one word. So, even without the found object being named, you have a great deal of information. In English, 'find' by itself tells us nothing about what is found. The English word needs surrounding words to tell who is doing the finding, what is being found, and when the action is taking place.

There is an interesting mention of a classificatory verb in the book, *The Shadow of Sequoyah: Social Documents of the Cherokee, 1862-1964,* by Anna and Jack Frederick Kilpatrick. The volume contains a letter from 1862, in which a young Cherokee soldier is complaining about someone having taken salt from him. The letter was written in syllabary, but it appears in the book only in English translation. In a description of the letter, the authors say that they can tell from the Cherokee verb that the salt was not granular, but was in bar form.[1] So, even though the letter did not specifically name a bar of salt, the verb would lead readers to picture it.

Care needs to be taken when interpreting classificatory verbs, but even very common English phrases like 'you all,' need to be understood thoroughly in order to be translated into Cherokee. In English, 'You all come back,' can be said to two or more people, and sometimes even to one person. As we have seen, though, Cherokee is very specific. If you were speaking to one person, you would say ᏔᎵᎥᎦᎢ *ihedolvi,* 'You (one) come back.' Talking to two people would be ᏙᏍᎥᎦᎢ *isdedolvi,* 'You two come back,' and to three or more, ᏗᎥᎦᎢ *itsedolvi,* 'You all come back.' Unlike

English verbs, Cherokee verbs draw clear pictures of situations and the number of people involved.

If you are only looking at the surface of Cherokee words, trying to match them exactly to English, there are so many ways to go wrong. I speak from experience. I remember when I had been taking online classes for a short time, I came across a video in Cherokee about how to make a peanut butter sandwich.[2] In the video, a Cherokee speaker narrated the process of making a sandwich. I understood very little of what was said—okay, almost nothing—but I did hear the words ᎤᎦᎾᏍᏓ ᎦᏅᎵᏰᏗ *uganasda ganvliyedi*. I knew that ᎤᎦᎾᏍᏓ *uganasda* meant 'sweet,' and together the two words must mean 'jelly,' or 'jam,' I reasoned. These two words were followed by ᎤᏂᏖᎸᎳᏗ *unitelvladi*, the Cherokee word for 'grapes.' That meant that ᎤᎦᎾᏍᏓ ᎦᏅᎵᏰᏗ ᎤᏂᏖᎸᎳᏗ *uganasda ganvliyedi unitelvladi* was referring to grape jelly or jam. I made a picture in my mind of a pile of gooey food being *ganvliyedi*. I shared my amazing insight with Ed, thinking how impressed he would be that I was now thinking in Cherokee, only to be very kindly redirected. He showed me what it meant with a hand motion which I understood as spreading something. *Ganvliyedi* did not actually describe any substance, but what you did with it. In other words, it was to be spread. I remember this was a relevatory moment for me. I realized then that I had been working from the English perspective. From then on, I started looking at Cherokee words differently.

Later, I found a listing for the word in the *Dictionary of the Cherokee Language*, compiled by J.T.Alexander. The word ᎦᏅᎵᏰᏗ *ganvlieyedi* was defined as, 'salve,' 'rub' and 'smear.'[3] Those were all things that could be spread on, so it made sense. This added even more layers to my understanding of the word, and to how I might use it in the future.

I was interested to later come across this word in *Cherokee Reference Grammar* by Brad Montgomery-Anderson: ᎤᏅᏗ ᎠᏔᏍᎩᏍᎩ ᏙᏣᏓᎸ ᎦᏅᎵᏰᏗ *unvdi atasgisgi dots(a)dalv ganvliyedi*, 'You rub milkweed on sores,' or, 'Milkweed is to be rubbed on sores.' Here, it was clear that rubbing went slightly beyond the idea of just spreading something.[4]

My view of the word was further expanded when I came across this passage in Mark 9:49, which used ᏏᎤᎵᏰᏗ *ganvliyedi* and another form of the word also: ᎨᎯᏴZ ᎠᏂᏋ ᎧᏗ ᎠᏛ ᏆᎯᎤᎵᏰᏗ ᏆᏎᎦᏗ, ᏙᏈ ᎯᏏ ᎠᏂᏋ-ᏆᏫᎦᏗ ᎠᏛ ᏏᎤᎵᏰᏗ ᏆᏎᎦᏗ *naniv-ye/h/no* ('and they') *atsilv* ('fire') *gvdi* ('using') *ama* ('salt') *getsinvliyedi* ('salted, spread, covered') *gesesdi* ('it will be') *ale* ('and') *nigav* ('all') *atsilv-gelasdi* ('sacrifice') *ama* ('salt') *ganvliyedi* ('salted, spread, covered') *gesesdi* ('it will be'). 'For everyone shall be salted with fire and every sacrifice will be salted with salt.' (*The Cherokee New Testament, Parallel Cherokee & English*).[5] Clearly, being salted with fire and being salted with salt are not only terribly unpleasant thoughts, but are also very different from spreading jelly on bread.

I realized that my idea of spreading was too narrow, and too dependent on the English meaning of the word. It might be more useful to think of evenly distributing something over something else. Studying the word opened up many possibilities, and I would not be surprised to come across more ways to think about the word in the future. And to think my interest was awakened by a video in Cherokee about how to make a peanut butter sandwich.

Words in Cherokee can also have a number of meanings just as English words do. In English, the word 'opening' can refer to a physical space, a hole, or it can mean an opportunity, among other things. In Cherokee, the noun, ᎤᏓᎤᏅ *udlanvdv*, is a space or an opening, such as a hole in a fence. If you say ᎤᏓᎤᎭ *udlanvda*, though, (noting the different ending), you are saying, 'there is an opening,' which might even describe a job opportunity. There is also another verb form, ᎤᏓᎤᏓᏕᎭ *udlanvdadeha*, which means, 'he or she has time,' and you can see that it talks about a space, or an opening in time.

Understanding can be deepened by searching the *Cherokee New Testament* for related words. For example, in Mark 4:32 we read the following: ᏥᏍᏆ ᎤᏓᎤᏅ ᎠᎭZᏪᏫᏙ *tsisqua udlanvda aninohilidohi.* The literal translation of this is: 'bird, an opening, they fly.' It is the translation for 'the fowls of the air.'

In Revelation 9:2 we read: ᎤᎥᏃ Ꮤ ᎡᏳ ᏙᏏ ᏍᏃᏍᏆᎬ ᎤᏍᎤᏍᏛ ᏍᏈᏅᏟ *nvdo/h/no iga ehi ale ganolesgv udlanvdv dulisihvsvgi.* The literal translation would be: 'and the sun and the air, an opening, they were darkened.' The translation is, 'and the sun and the air were darkened.' This is particularly interesting because in order to write about air that could be darkened, it had to be given a location in space, *udlanvdv.*

Along those same lines, in the *Cherokee New Testament,* I came across this: Revelation 21:21: ᏒᏬᏍᏥᏏ ᎤᏍᎤᏛ ᏎᏕ *edasdiyi udlanvdv gaduhv.* This is Cherokee for 'the street of the city.' ᏒᏬᏍᏥᏏ *edasdiyi* means 'a place to go' or 'pathway.' ᎤᏍᎤᏛ *udlanvdv,* 'an opening,' and ᏎᏕ *gaduhv* is the Cherokee word for 'city.' So, the street of the city is described as an opening that is a pathway. There are other words to say 'street' in Cherokee, but this phrase paints a vivid picture.

It's important to look beyond the first dictionary definition you find for a Cherokee word. If you can see the word in different contexts over time, you will be deepening your knowledge of Cherokee. Understanding the related words and the pictures they are conveying will help broaden your ability to communicate ideas in speech and writing, and to comprehend what you hear and read.

Students in Ed Fields' classes find out early on that Cherokee words are very descriptive. Hearing that ᏣᎳ *svg(a)ta,* 'apple,' actually means, 'it is hanging,' helps to shift the new learner into the Cherokee way of thinking. It may not be easy to track down what every single Cherokee word depicts, but it's good to get into the habit of thinking about meanings and what the words are actually picturing.

Take the word, ᏥᏳ *tsiyu,* for example. ᏥᏳ *tsiyu* means 'canoe,' and more recently added meanings are 'boat' and 'airplane.' An alert student may try to understand the full meaning by considering what a canoe, a boat, and an airplane have in common. Transportation, perhaps? But then, wouldn't ᏥᎬ *tsiyu* apply to bicycles, cars, trucks and buses also? It doesn't.

To understand the word, it's helpful to travel back in time. If you don't have a time machine handy, you can look to history. Like many other tribes, Cherokees made dugout canoes from hardwood trees, including the Tulip Poplar or Tuliptree, also known as a Yellow Poplar, perhaps because of the butter-yellow color its leaves turn in autumn. The Tulip Poplar was particularly well-suited to canoe making, since the tree was very straight and could grow to well over ninety feet tall. The trunks have few lower branches, making it easier to fashion into canoes. Also, the wood was not prone to warping, and fewer tools were needed to cut boards because of the height and straightness of the trees.[6]

I am personally very familiar with the Tulip Poplar, as there were many where I grew up in Virginia. In fact, there was a tree behind our house, so tall and majestic that, as children, we named it Mr. Joe. Well, maybe the name Mr. Joe doesn't conjure majestic visions for most adults, but children think differently. The huge circumference of his trunk made Mr. Joe a favorite meeting place for neighborhood children. A number of us could sit behind his trunk for secret, highly-classified meetings about important kid stuff, and the adults were none the wiser. The lowest branches hung down far enough for us to pick the beautiful tulip-like flowers in the spring, but the branches themselves began much too high up for anyone to climb. This long vertical rise before the branches began also contributed to its popularity for canoes. In fact, the Tulip Poplar tree is also called Canoe Tree or Canoewood by some.

Even more interesting, is the fact that ᏥᎬ *tsiyu* is also the Cherokee word for Tulip Poplar.

Now, when you consider *tsiyu* as meaning canoe, boat, plane and Tulip Poplar, new ideas other than transportation may come to mind. What are the qualities they all have in common? Before thinking of an answer, consider another related word, ᏥᎬᎪᏗ *tsiyuk(o)di*, meaning 'straight,' as in direction. Consider also the word, SGAႨT *duyuk(o)dvi*, 'the truth.' Could there be any connection? It's not necessary to draw any definite conclusions. On the contrary, it might be more useful to keep the images of what these words represent together in your mind. If you think of the relatedness of the images, rather than trying to pin one word to one meaning, you might get closer to feeling what it is like to think in Cherokee. If you think about it, how do children learn the full meanings of words? An English-speaking child may first hear the word 'fork' when eating, but they will later come across 'a fork in the road,' 'pitchfork,' 'tuning fork,' and the expression, 'to fork it over.' They will learn these different meanings naturally over time, in their immersed environments. And they will intuitively come to understand what the different words have in common. Most second-language learners don't have the opportunity to drop into an immersed twenty-four hours a day environment where everyone in their home and community is speaking Cherokee. But we can all search for words that interest us and experience some of what children experience when they are learning naturally at home. Let your interests be your guide on the great adventure of learning Cherokee.

◆ ◆ ◆

I have heard people say that Cherokee just isn't a language that can express subtlety of thought. Some think it is just too exact and literal. I would challenge anyone who thinks that way to begin reading the Bible translated into Cherokee. You will find detailed stories which can form a model for your own writing. Save passages that speak to you and hold your interest.

I have a desktop folder titled "NewT" (though it has many passages from the Old Testament also), where I save interesting words and verses I have come across. Many times, I will look up words after Ed mentions something in class. Sometimes, I will be writing in Cherokee, and looking for a particular word that isn't in the dictionary, or searching for a way to say a phrase. Other times, I will come across a word that just strikes me, for whatever reason. I write the word and example sentences, and keep them in a file. If it comes from the *Cherokee New Testament*, it goes into "NewT." Here are a few of my "NewT" files names: 'Bible-have living thing,' 'evangelist,' 'In times past,' 'door,' 'Blessing,' 'sift,' 'Beautiful thoughts,' 'About suffering,' 'usquaniktane/usquan- ikdi,' 'Boat words,' 'Sailing,' 'nudvhnadega,' 'ᏎᏍᎤᏘᏍᏍ,' 'Brothers,' 'Brethern,' 'ᎠᎵᎦᏬ,' 'Carried him away lead him away,' and 'Hidden Heart,' among many others. These files serve as treasured resources that I draw upon when I am working on writing, or just thinking about words. When I come across new passages or other materials related to the file words, I add them in. The passages come from a wide range of verses, full of rich detail. If you want to see what the Cherokee language is capable of, study the Bible in Cherokee and other old stories and documents.

If people object to reading Bible verses for any reason—it goes against their spiritual beliefs, or perhaps they reject what they see as a religion which they feel was forced upon the Cherokees—I urge them to reconsider. First of all, every reader is capable of reading critically and separating the message—or religious content—from the language, if they so desire. Some may ask, why would someone want to read a book whose content doesn't interest them? I would answer that Bible translations, some of which began even before the syllabary was created by Sequoyah, offer a treasury of vocabulary and examples of usage unavailable anyplace else.

I have often made good use of old documents, the Bible in Cherokee, and other resources. Some years ago I became interested in translating and recording a song that had been very popular when I was a child. The song was sung in Japanese and was called *Ue O Muite Arukou*, 'I Look Up As I Walk,' and the English words to the song were widely available. It concerns a young man who is broken-hearted and thinks back to happier times. The song is simple, but uses poetic language and is very touching. One line in particular that spoke of a heart filled with sorrow caught my attention. I wanted to be able to get that across in Cherokee. Cherokee is such a precise and literal language that I wondered how such emotion could be expressed and still make sense.

It's important to establish what is meant by literal and non-literal language. Literal language means what it says, with no hidden meaning. Non-literal, or figurative language, on the other hand, is language which suggests meaning beyond the surface meaning of the words. One example of figurative language is a simile, which is a comparison of two unlike things using 'like' or 'as.' When you say a child is like a flower, the comparison makes you think of flower-like qualities a child may have, such as softness and beauty. If you say a child is a flower, however, you are using a different figure of speech, a metaphor, which makes a comparison without using 'like' or 'as.' It is much more powerful and direct. I knew I would need figurative language to describe a heart filled with sorrow, as in the song I wanted to translate. But a heart is being talked about as if it were a vessel of some sort which could be filled with feelings. Was it possible to use this sort of language in Cherokee? Were there any precedents? I knew I needed to research.

I turned first to the website of the "Digital Archive of Indigenous Language Persistence" (DAILP), where original Cherokee documents are archived. I came across a letter from 1951 written by a young man in jail to his mother. He had someone helping him, as he was still learning to write in syllabary. The letter was signed: DB ᏍᏍᏗᏥᎾ ᏍᏍᎥᏩᏟᏍ *ayv osdigina osdo/h/welvga*, 'This was written by us calves.' Clearly, they are not young calves, or young animals. But the metaphorical comparison gives you the idea of restless young men, full of energy, and it also adds a touch of humor.[7]

Searching further back in time to 1833, I found a passage in *Poor Sarah or The Indian Woman*, a religious tract which had been translated into Cherokee by Elias Boudinot. When Sarah was asked how her day had been, she responded: ᎯᏍᎣ ᏍᏴᏁ, ᎤᎦᏘ ᎤᏎᎭᏁ ᎡᏍᏍᏩᏟ ᏣᏢᏈ *nigadv osiyu, unah uganasiyu esgaquo wadulisi*, 'All good; sweeter than honey.' Sarah compares her day to honey. It would make no sense literally—a day is a measure of time, and has no qualities of taste—but the use of figurative language makes the meaning clear. It was a wonderful and enjoyable day.[8]

My research showed then, that Cherokee does have a tradition of using figurative language, and I would be able to use similar language when translating. Now, I needed to think about how to talk about a heart filled with sorrow.

When I first looked up 'heart' in the *Cherokee-English Dictionary* I found some surprising things. I had heard the word ᎤᏓᏅᏙ *udanvdo*, 'his or her heart,' but I also found the word ᎤᎾᎯᏫ *una/h/wi* 'heart,' the bodily organ. There was also a reference to ᎤᎾᎯᏫ ᏘᏦᏗ ᏧᏍᎦᎶᎦ *una/h/wi itsusdi tsugaloga*, 'heart shaped leaves,' clearly talking about the shape of the organ. My first thought was that I wouldn't be using ᎤᎾᎯᏫ *una/h/wi* for my translation since it referred to the actual heart.

I broadened my search by looking into the Old and New Testaments for passages that mentioned the word 'heart.' I was particularly struck by this passage in Luke 2:51: ᎤᏥᏏᎩᏂ ᎯᎠ ᎾᏍᎩ ᏂᎦᏛ ᎤᏍᏆᏂᎦᏗᎭᏫᏒᎵ ᎤᎾᎯᏫᏱ *utsisgini hia nasgi nigadv usquanig(o)tane una/h/wiyi*, 'But his mother kept all these sayings in her heart.' It interested me to find that Cherokee language had a way to talk about things being stored in the heart.

The word ᎤᎾᎯᏫᏱ *una/h/wiyi* was used for 'in her heart.' When the verse says Mary 'kept all these sayings in her heart,' it was her response to finding her son, Jesus, sitting among teachers and other learned men who were astonished at the child's wisdom. She didn't comprehend what she saw, yet she knew it was extraordinary and something to be quietly treasured in her heart, having faith that she would understand some day. Even though the passage used the word for the anatomical heart, it was using it in a metaphorical way, as if the heart were a place where thoughts and feelings could be stored.

Next, I found this passage in Ephesians 4:18: ᎤᏓᎶᏏᏍᏙᏗᏍᎬᎥ ᏧᏂᎾᎯᏫ ᏗᏍᏓᏯᎢᏳ ᎨᏒᎢ *nvdigalisdodisgv tsunina/h/wi disdayiyu gesvi*, 'because of the blindness of their heart.' This was interesting because it used the word for the bodily heart, but now was saying a bodily heart could be blind. However, looking closely at the word, we find the Cherokee is not saying 'blind,' but rather, ᏗᏍᏓᏱᏳ *disdayiyu*, 'they (their hearts) are hard.' The heart itself being hardened is a metaphor for being closed off and unfeeling. This showed there could be some crossover of the two different ways to say 'heart.' How else could ᎤᏓᏅᏙ *adanvdo*, 'a heart,' be used? I wondered.

I found an example of what I was looking for in *Poor Sarah*: ᎾᏍᎩ ᏄᏍᏛ ᎦᏓᏅᏝᎬ ᎠᏆᏓᏅᏔᏫ *nahsgi nusdv gadanvtesgv aquadanvtv*, 'I think this in my heart.' [9] Here, the heart refers to her innermost self.

I also found this passage, which expresses strong emotions in Ephesians 5:19: ᏕᏥᏃᎩᏍᎬᏍᏗ ᏙᏗᏣᏛᏅᏔᏫ ᏗᏓᎴᏫᏍᎬᏍᏗ ᎤᎬᏫᏳᎯ ᏕᏥᏃᎩᏍᏗᏍᎬᏍᏗ *detsinogisgesdi doditsadanvtv didalehvsgesdi ugvwiyuhi detsinogisdisgesdi*, 'singing and making melody in your heart to the Lord.' ᏙᏗᏣᏛᏅᏔᏫ *doditsadanvtv*, 'in your heart,' is a form of ᎤᏓᏅᏙ *udanvdo*.

Numerous examples from the Old and the New Testament could be given to show almost parallel use of forms of ᎤᎾᎥᏗ *una/h/wiyi* and ᎤᏓᏅᏙ *udanvdo*. But in my reading, I found important differences between the two words. For example, ᎤᎾᎥ *una/h/wi* was used to talk about having love in your heart for others. Also, in 1 Peter 1:22 we read: ᎤᎵᏂᎩᏛ ᏕᏣᏓᎨᏳᏎᏍᏗ ᎢᏧᏗᏍᎨᏍᏗ ᎦᏓᎭ ᏂᎨᏒᎾ ᎢᏥᎾᎥ *ulinigidv detsadageyusesdi itsvdisgesdi gadaha nigesvna itsina/h/wi*, 'see that ye love one another with a pure heart fervently' (*itsina/h/wi*, 'your hearts'). As of yet, I haven't found ᎤᏓᏅᏙ *udanvdo* being used in the same way.

The word ᎤᏓᏅᏙ *udanvdo* also had meanings that ᎤᎾᎥᏗ *una/h/wiyi* did not. In Genesis 12:13 we find: ᏗᏆᏓᏅᏙᏃ ᎬᏁᏍᏗ ᏂᎯ ᏔᏣᏂᏌᏛ *aquadanvdo/h/no gvnesdi nihi itsvnisadv*, 'and my soul hath lived for thy sake.' ᏗᏆᏓᏅᏙ *aquadanvdo*, is 'my soul.' (*The Cherokee Old Testament (in Part): Parallel Cherokee and English*). [10] And in John 1:32 we find ᎤᏓᏅᏙ *adanvdo* as a translation for 'Spirit': ᎠᎩᎪᎲᎩ ᎠᏓᏅᏙ ᎫᎴ-ᏗᏍᎪᏂᎯ ᎾᏍᎩᏯ ᏓᏳᏁᏢᏅᎩ ᎦᎸᎳᏗ *agigohvgi adanvdo gule-disgo/h/nihi nasgiya dayunetlunvgi galvladi*, 'I saw the Spirit descending from heaven like a dove.' In Luke 4:1, 'Holy Ghost,' is translated as ᎦᎸᏉᏗᏳ ᎠᏓᏅᏙ *galvquodiyu adanvdo*, with ᎦᎸᏉᏗᏳ *galvquodiyu* having the meaning of 'holy' or 'sacred.' ᎤᎾᏫ *una/h/wi* could not follow into that spiritual territory.

A clear division between the two terms appears in Mark 12:33: ᎾᏍᎩᏃ ᎠᏓᎨᏳᏗᏱ ᎬᏙᏗᏱ ᏂᎬ ᎣᎾᏫᏱ, ᎠᎴ ᏂᎬ ᎠᏓᏅᏖᏗᏱ, ᎠᎴ ᏂᎬ ᎠᏓᏅᏙ *nasgi/h/no adageyudiyi gvdodiyi nikv ona/h/wiyi, ale nikv adanvtediyi, ale nikv adanvdo*, 'And to love him with all the heart, and with all the understanding, and with all the soul.' 'One's heart,' encompassing human emotions, is translated as ᎣᎾᏫᏱ *ona/h/wiyi*, and 'the soul,' is ᎠᏓᏅᏙ *adanvdo.*

Although I started my research being surprised that ᎤᎾᏫᏱ *una/h/wiyi* and ᎤᏓᏅᏙ *udanvdo* seemed almost interchangeable, I soon saw a clear line beyond which ᎤᎾᏫᏱ *una/h/wiyi* could not go: the sacred.

Interestingly, the use of ᎤᎾᏫ *una/h/wi* has narrowed since the New Testament was translated in the 1800s. It is rarely used today except for the most technical reference to the actual heart. ᎤᏓᏅᏙ *udanvdo*, on the other hand, has broadened in use, and is often the only word for 'heart' that students learn. It can even be used to refer to the bodily heart, as in the following *Cherokee-English Dictionary* sentence: "ᎤᏓᏅᏙ ᎤᎴᏫᏍᏓᏁᎸᎢ *udanhdo ulehwisdanelvi* 'His heart stopped on him.'"[11]

Now, back to what started this exploration: how to talk about the heart and emotions in Cherokee. I had found similarities and differences in the two words for 'heart,' but was curious how they would line up with different meanings of 'heart' in English. When I started listing what 'heart' could mean, it became clear that the English word 'heart had a lot in common with both ᎤᎾᏫᏱ *una/h/wiyi* and ᎤᏓᏅᏙ *udanvdo.* All three words could be used to talk about strong emotions, the innermost self and the physical heart. In addition, the

English word 'heart' carries other meanings that do no apply to the Cherokee words: location, as in, 'in the heart of the city'; centrality, as in 'the heart of the matter'; courage, as in, 'take heart'; memory, as in, 'to learn by heart'; and the inner leaves of a vegetable such as celery heart or artichoke heart. Also, 'heart,' and the Cherokee word ᎤᏍᏓᏩᏗ *una/h/wiyi* can both be used to talk about love for others, love of God, and to refer to something that is heart-shaped.

An interesting note is that 'heart' in English does not usually refer to the spirit or to the soul. Of the three words, 'heart,' ᎤᏍᏓ *una/h/wi*, and ᎤᏓᏅᏙ *udanvdo*, only the last refers to spirit and soul. See Figure 8.1 to visualize the comparison of 'heart,' ᎤᏍᏓ *una/h/wi*, and ᎤᏓᏅᏙ *udanvdo*.

Figure 8.1. Heart Diagram

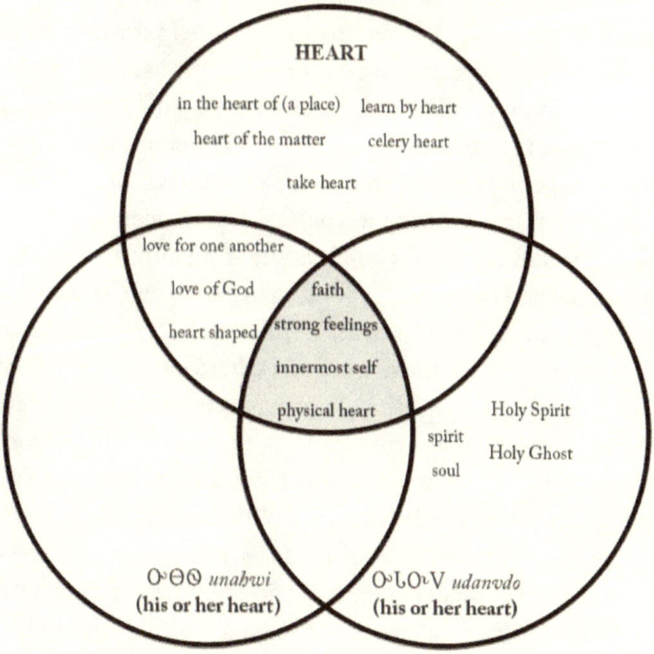

Getting back to my translation, I determined that ᎤᏍᏓ *un-*

a/h/wi would work best since it is clearly tied to feelings of love. My research had shown that Cherokee is not always literal, but that there was a tradition going back to at least the early 1800s of using figurative language. So imagining the heart as a vessel that can be filled with feelings, good or bad, is within that tradition. I found that ᎣᏏ ᎠᏞᎤᏞᏓᏍᎤᏗ *uyo adanvdadisdi* could express the idea of sorrow since it carries the idea of being reminded of sad things. And since I had found evidence of metaphorical phrasing in Cherokee, I decided to translate 'sorrow filled my heart,' as ᎣᏏ ᎠᏞᎤᏞᏓᏍᎤᏗ ᎣᏍᏃᏛ ᎠᏬᎾ *uyo adanvdadisdi ukalitsv agina/h/wi*. With patient research I was able to translate the song into Cherokee, confident that I was using the language in a way that followed tradition. I titled my Cherokee version of the song, ᏃᏉᏏ ᏚᎦᏎᎯᎭ *noqu(i)si degasehiha*, 'I am Counting the Stars.' (You can listen to a recording of the song here: https://youtu.be/5xfmL1QQkaQ).[12]

Being able to sing and record the song was very meaningful to me. When singing a song in Cherokee, or listening to one, you are learning to attach emotions and complex memories to Cherokee words. Most songs are written to make you feel something. They can make you laugh or make you feel joy or deep sadness. They do this through an artful combination of melody and words. The song I translated describes a young man counting the stars to help him keep from crying. His heart is filled with sorrow. Think about what it means to hear those words in Cherokee.

Just as a song in English may bring up memories and feelings, a song in Cherokee may bring forth pictures and feelings from the past. Listening to a song in Cherokee will lead you to associate the sound of Cherokee words with your own experiences, rather than with the English translation of those words. Ask yourself, 'What might Cherokee speakers see, feel and think when they hear the word ᏃᏉᏏ *noqu(i)si*?' They might see a glittering night sky, but each will see a different sky, overlaid with his or her memories and emotions. The whole song will elicit a wide range of mental pictures and feelings, personal to each listener. But none of the speakers will be thinking of the word 'star.'

When I hear the word ZƱb *noqu(i)si*, I might recall lying in the grass and looking up at the night sky when I was a very small child. I might remember the feeling of smallness beneath the vast sky, and the comforting wall of sound made by crickets and tree frogs. I might remember another night when I was around twenty and visiting a friend who had a cabin by the water. I was far from the city and the sky was bright with stars. There was phosphorescence on the water so that it sparkled almost as if it were reflecting the sky. I felt a quiet beauty and peace there that I've carried with me ever since. I could also recall a winter midnight some years ago when I stepped outside on the porch to look up at the stars, and to be alone with the grief I was feeling at the time. I can vividly recall the beauty of the glittering stars and the loneliness they seemed to reflect back at me. These memories and countless more may be called up when I hear the word ZƱb *noqu(i)si*. Cherokee words become associated with my emotions, thoughts and with my entire life. They become part of me.

When second-language learners listen to songs in Cherokee, they have the chance to experience the words from inside the Cherokee world. Listen to the words, and sing if you can, and let the sound of Cherokee flood your mind with pictures and complex memories and thoughts. They will be unique to you. This is a world away from seeing the words and writing the English equivalents.

Learning Cherokee is a lifelong journey for me, and maybe, for you too. If so, your understanding will become more profound over time as you read, write, listen, converse, sing and perhaps even joke in Cherokee.

When you make the language an authentic part of your life, words and phrases will spark memories, pictures, emotions and ideas, rather than flashcard translations into English. That is called thinking in Cherokee and that is what I aim for. I hope you will too.

CHAPTER NINE

Translation in Action

ED FIELDS AND MARY RAE

ᏏᏲ ᏂᎦᏛ *siyo nigadv*, 'hello, all of you,' I am glad you are here. In February 2022, Meli and I worked together, by telephone, to translate the epigraph, 'Start and don't stop. What you do after start determines how fast, how much and how well you learn.' We recorded the call on each end of the phone line, transcribed it, cut it to fit this chapter and so it is shared here. I have included my commentary about certain parts of it in hopes my comments help you.

E: I'm going to do it a little at a time here. (I guess before we get too far along, I should tell you about a term I use throughout—'bounce,' 'bouncing,' 'bounced.' I'm not sure I can explain 'bounce' as that's my term for it. I guess if you were a musician or a mechanic you might say that you're 'tuning' or 'fine-tuning.' A musician tunes their instrument to get it to a place they like. A mechanic tunes a motor to get it to a place they like. So in my mind I tune or fine-tune, I 'bounce' sounds that fine-tune meanings looking for the Cherokee word or version of it I like.)

M: *hawa* 'Okay.'

E: First one . . . 'Start and don't stop.' *halena hesdi tsihalewistani.*
(halena hesdi tsihalewistani was not quite right, but you have to
start somewhere, have to put something out there to begin with,
so I started with that. I knew *halena* was the word I wanted.
But *hesdi* and *tsihalewistani* were not quite right. *hesdi* was close
though, so I began to use *hesdi* to 'bounce' with, figuring I'd
replace *tsihalewistani* once I get the word that's similar to *hesdi.*
I'm just going to do it one word at a time.)

M: *halena hesdi* . . . what are you using for stop—wouldn't you use
like *tsisuligotsi?*

E: Okay (I mean I'll put my bouncing of *hesdi* aside for a little while
to deal with *tsisuligotsi.*) So, *halena hesdi tsihisulgoi,* something
like that (I say *tsihisulgoi* as it is spoken, that is, I leave out the
vowel, as I have not yet decided if the vowel after '*l*' is '*i*' or '*a.*'
And it needs bounced.)

M: Let me just say one thing here. You're using *halena,* so it's like
you're speaking to one person instead of speaking to everybody.
I kind of like that, because I feel like the reader, you know, it's
more personal to the reader. But, yeah, I like saying *halena.*

E: Yeah. That second word 'don't stop' is what's throwing me. It's
a little different than *halewisda.*

M: Yeah, because that's like stopping something that's in motion.
What about—I think this is what you were saying, it would be
tsihisuligotsi.

E: *halena ale hesdi tsihisulgotsi.* (And *tsihisulgotsi* will need
bounced.)

M: *tsihisulagotsi.* Is it *tsihisuligotsi?*

E: (I'm still bouncing for *hesdi*) *hisulgoi* is the word (to answer Meli's question, I bounce off a similar word. I bounce off *tsihisulgo* to get to the similar word *hisulgoi.* Then I go back to trying to capture my former thought of that word similar to *hesdi.*)

M: *hisuligoi.*

E: I'm going to have to write that down, *hisulgoi.* (It's not the word I'm looking for, I'm writing it down so that I can see the syllabary writings to look at it to get to the word I'm looking for, looking at the ending of the word, or the suffix as they call it. While I write it in syllabary I pronounce the sounds slowly, letting them talk to me. I'm still looking for the word I want to find, the one that's similar to *hesdi,* but also trying to get to the meaning for 'start and don't stop.' Writing gave me time to think. Writing in syllabary was also familiar and helped because it was familiar. Plus writing brings more of your senses to the task, you can feel and see and hear as you pronounce under your breath or whisper out loud or even talk to yourself as you write. Then I say to Meli,) *halena hesdi hisulgoi.*

M: *hi-su-li-go-i.*

E: (I slowly bounce sounds off the word *hisulgoi,* trying to get the word similar to *hisulgoi,* so I can go back to bouncing for the word similar to *hesdi,* I say to Meli) It could be '*li*' or '*la,*' depends. (Then I bounce the sounds of the syllables as I listen and let them talk to me) *hesdi tsihisulgo . . . hesdi tsihisulgoi.* Okay.

M: Aha.

E: Let's try that. *hesdi tsihisulgoi . . .* (But the ending part, the suffix of *tsihisulgoi* wasn't quite working out for me.).

M: You're saying . . . *tsihisulagoi?*

E: Nooo (I mean that I'm not saying that's the word I'm looking for. I'm looking for the word similar to it), let me think about this a minute in quiet. (I was looking for two words—the word that was similar to *hesdi* and the word that was similar to *tsihisulgoi*. I needed quiet because sometimes the slightest sound or distraction can stop or hinder the word that's on the tip of your brain from coming. And sometimes you've only heard a word once or a long time ago when you were a little child and an elder said the word, and you're concentrating to bring that word to mind. Some Cherokee words aren't in a dictionary or word list. You have to give the Cherokee words time to talk to you, to tell you about themselves, to get to know them, to allow them to paint a picture, to picturize. And quiet can help with that. I needed to let the words come. So I begin to pronounce beneath my breath, trying out versions while listening to the sounds and thinking of the meanings.)

M: *hawa* 'Okay.'

E: Okay, how's this one? *hesdi tsihisulgotsvi.*

M: *hesdi tsihisuligotsvi.*

E: *hesdi tsihisulgotsvi . . . hesdi tsihisulagotsvi . . .* (I'm checking the sounds.)

M: You're saying *hesdi tsihisulagotsvi?*

E: It ain't *'li'*.

M: Ah *hawa* 'okay.'

E: *hesdi tsihisulgotsvi.*

M: *hawa* 'Okay.'

E: I think.

M: *halena hesdi tsihisulagotsvi.*

E: Yeah, that sounds good.

M: Uh huh *osda* 'It's good.'

E: *hesdi tsihisul(a)gotsvi*, that's what it sounds like (I'm still saying it like a speaker says it, by dropping the vowel *'a'*. The *'(a)'* in the phonetics here shows that the vowel is silent. That word *tsihisul(a) gotsvi* is the one I was looking for, the one that sounded similar to *tsihisulgoi*, that had a different suffix *'tsvi.'* Now I just needed the word that was similar to *hesdi*.) *halena ale hesdi tsihisul(a) gotsvi*. I better write that down.

M: *vv ayasquu* 'Yes, me too.' [We both laugh]

E: (I'm writing *halena ale hesdi tsihisul(a)gotsvi* in syllabary, pronouncing each of the words slowly, drawing out the sounds as I listen to them) *he-s. . . tlesdi* (I started to say *hesdi* when *tlesdi* came. *tlesdi* is the one similar to *hesdi* I had been searching for.) I know what it is—*tlesdi.*

M: *hawa* 'Okay.' *tlesdi. halena ale tlesdi tsihisul(a)gotsvi.*

E: *tlesdi tsihisulagotsvi . . . halena tlesdi tsihisul(a)gotsvi.* (I'm saying it both ways here, with and without the vowel. I'm just making sure). Okay. Got *halena tlesdi tsihisul(a)gotsvi.*

M: Are you saying *tlesdi* or *hesdi?*

E: *tlesdi. halena ale tlesdi tsihisul(a)gotsvi.*

M: *tlesdi tsihisul(a)gotsvi. hawa* 'Okay.'

E: So, 'start running and don't stop.'

M: I'm trying, Ed! I got my running shoes on!

[We both laugh]

E: So that's the word. Now, what else?

M: 'What you do after start determines how fast, how much and how well you learn.' So, guess we're thinking about what you do after 'start.' So, it's kind of like, everything that you do . . . if you're talking about everything that you'd be doing you might say, let me see . . . yeah, I'm trying to think . . . how to put it together. What if you said like . . . 'thinking of everything that you will be doing' . . . or 'that you could be doing' . . . *nasgi* . . . *yidetsalvwisdanehesdi* . . . 'everything that you might be doing that you could be doing?' It's just like, the parts of the sentence you have to—I'm thinking like, now how would you put those together, you're not going to necessarily say it in that order, like 'what you do after start,' you know?

E: Yeah, I'm drawing a blank here.

M: Does that make any sense though?

E: Yes. It means, I lost the thoughts.

M: [Meli laughs] No! I meant, did what *I* said make any sense? Could you say, *nasgi yidetsalvwisdanehesdi*, 'all that you will be doing, working on?'

E: No, what you're saying is 'now keep working,' something like that. (I misheard her. Phones sometimes do not let you hear clear enough. In *yidetsalvwisdanehesdi*, the '*yi*' is saying 'if' and *yidetsalvwisdanehesdi* by itself sounds to me like it means 'if you keep working at it' or 'if you keep working.' *nasgi* added to it sounds to me like it means 'that is if you are going to be working' or something like that. I've seen other meanings for *nasgi*, it depends on contextual usage.)

M: *vv* 'Yes.' *nasgi detsalvwisdaneha?*

E: 'Now, you are working.' You were sitting there a few minutes ago and now, you're working.

[We both laugh]

E: (Since I don't have a dictionary handy, I ask) What's the word for determine?

M: Let me see. The word for determine, can that be used for other than like a person?

E: I need a definition.

M: Oh, what's—in English?

E: Yes.

M: I think you might say 'decide,' it decides what's going to happen. Let me look up 'determine.' 'Cause something to occur in a particular way, be the decisive factor in.' So I think it kind of decides it?

E: Kind of decides.

M: Well, it will decide. But can you use deciding that way . . . the verb for deciding isn't that like—what's the word for deciding or to be decided, *digugdodi* or something? But can that be—this isn't like a person deciding. It's like what you do will decide.

E: (*digugdodi* is not quite right, so I bounce the word, then say) *da-gu-go-ta-ni*, right? *dagug(o)tani*. (I say it like it's written with the vowel, then like it's spoken without the vowel, but to show that in phonetic written form you put the vowel like this *'(o)'* which means the *'o'* is not pronounced.)

M: *dagug(o)tani* . . . okay. Well, can you use it in that way, if it's like saying 'the things that you do will decide'?

E: Yeah. (*dagug(o)tani* can mean that—'it will decide'—but 'you' isn't in there yet, it will need bounced. In my mind I'm bouncing words, but manage to say) Thinking here (to let Meli know I'll need quiet for a little while. Almost thirty-nine seconds go by.)

M: What is it you're thinking of?

E: (I've been thinking of a lot, and tell her the findings) I got *iyusdi* (but since I like the older word for it better, I'm going to use the older word) I got *dagug(o)tani iyusdi/h/no* (the *'h'* in *iyusdi/h/no* is connecting to *'no'* so is a nasalized air *'hno'* sound like in the chart on page 80) *detsalvwisdanehv deha-*

del(o)/h/quasgv (the *'o'* in *dehadel(o)/h/quasgv* is silent, the *'l'* partners with the previous vowel *'e'* to become the sound *'del.'* The */h/* makes an air sound, the linguistics call this *intrusive h*. It won't show up when written in syllabary, ᏕᎭᏕᎶᏆᎧᎬ, but it can in phonetics like *'/h/'—dehadel(o)/h/quasgv.* See how the spoken and phonetically-written versions are not the same. In syllabary, the *intrusive h* is not written, all that is written is the syllable Ꮅ *'lo.'* So when you say this, or other ones that have a silent vowel or an *intrusive h*, then you would not pronounce the silent vowel but you would do the air sound for the *intrusive h*.)

M: *detsalvwisdanehv*. And what is after *detsalvwisdanehv*?

E: *dehadel(o)/h/quasgv.*

M: Are you saying *detsadel(o)/h/quasgv*?

E: *deha-*.

M: *deha-*, okay. I thought I misunderstood. *hawa* 'Okay.' *dagug(o)tani . . . dagugotani iyusdi/h/no detsalvwisdanehv dehadel(o)/h/quasgv*. Okay. 'Will decide.'

E: Say it again.

M: Is it *dagug(o)tani* or *dagugotani*?

E: *dagug(o)tani.*

M: *dagug(o)tani iyusdi/h/no detsalvwisdanehv dehadel(o)/h/quasgv.*

E: (I'm not quite satisfied with it, so do some bouncing, then tell Meli) *iyusdi/h/no detsalvwisdanehv dehadel(o)/h/quasgv dagug(o)tani.*

M: *dagug(o)tani* coming at the end now?

E: Not yet, (I'm thinking some more, and bouncing). That's just a phrase, we're not done yet.

M: I know, I meant [Meli laughs] I meant that it's—

E: When the bell goes off we know it's done.

M: [Meli laughs] I'll be listening—I'll be listening for that.

[We both laugh]

M: So, are you putting *dagug(o)tani* in front of *iyusdi/h/no*?

E: No, *iyusdi/h/no detsalvwisdanehv dehadel(o)/h/quasgv dagug(o)tani.*

M: Ah! *hawa* 'Okay!' *iyusdi/h/no detsalvwisdanehv dehadel(o)/h/quasgv dagug(o)tani. hawa* 'Okay.'

E: Okay, I'm going to run by it this time, see what it says. *iyusdi/h/no detsalvwisdanehv dehadel(o)/h/quasgv dagug(o)tani yiga hol/h/tsegvi.*

M: *siquu tsinihiwi,* 'Say it again.' *yiga?*

E: *yiga hol/h/tsegvi.*

M: *hol/h/tsegvi. yiga hol/h/tsegvi.*

E: 'How good you are learning.'

M: *vv osda* 'Yes, it's good.' That covers that.

E: So it won't be as 'fast' as in English, that's cause the more you understand, the more you're going to learn.

M: Uh huh.

E: So the more you understand, you covered that part, so you're going to learn more, and keep learning more, you know?

M: Uh huh.

E: If I said *nusvnula*, it sounds like it's guaranteed it's going to be fast.

M: Right.

E: So I don't guarantee.

[We both laugh]

M: I guess you could use *ahida*, which is 'you learn it easily.' Which doesn't necessarily say 'speed' but sort of gives the idea of, you know, it's coming easily.

E: Let's try *nahidv*. (*ahida* is like 'it is easy,' and *nahidv* is 'as it becomes easier.') *iyusdi/h/no detsalvwisdanehv dehadel(o)/h/quasgv dagug(o)tani* (I think about it for several seconds, then say) I could not put *nahidv* there anywhere at the moment.

M: *yiga nahidv osi/h/no?*

E: Yeah, (I mean, yeah I will think about what she said and see if something will come from it) I'm going to have to think about it again. New thoughts here. *iyusdi/h/no detsalvwisdanehv*

155

dehadel(o)/h/quasgv dagug(o)tani. (I think about it for several seconds, then) *osi*—no. (What I was thinking of didn't fit.) Let's see now.

M: Could be *osi*—*nahidv/h/no hol/h/tsegvi*, and then have *yigi* at the end or *yiga* at the end?

E: I'm going to—before I guarantee that, I'm going to need to figure it out here. *iyusdi/h/no detsalvwisdanehv dehadel(o)/h/quasgv dagug(o)tani yiga osi*—no, I couldn't put *nahidv* there anywhere. Go ahead and read it how you read it. (It can help you to hear someone else say or read back the words, you sort of can think 'does it makes sense or not?')

M: *iyusdi/h/no detsalvwisdanehv dehadel(o)/h/quasgv dagug(o)tani osi nahidv/h/no hol/h/tsegvi*—*yigi*. That's just changing it around, isn't it? Could you have *osi nahidv/h/no*?

E: (I'm focusing on what I'm writing in syllabary) I'm going to change that out here.

M: *hol/h/tsegvi yiga, yiga* at the end maybe?

E: Okay, I'm going to try this way now. *iyusdi/h/no detsalvwisdanehv dehadel(o)/h/quasgv dagug(o)tani* . . . and it still throws off when I put that in there, not that *nahidv* exactly. Try again then. *iyusdi/h/no detsalvwisdanehv dehadel(o)/h/quasgv dagug(o)tani nahidv hol/h/tsegvi.* (The words are trying to tell me something, and I need to listen, so I take time to listen to the sounds, to the words, letting them talk to me. To make them sure.) *iyusdi/hno detsalvwisdanehv dehadel(o)/h/quasgv dagug(o)tani nahidv hol/h/tsegvi.*

M: *yigi, yigv, yigi* after that? *nahidv holtsegvi yigi?*

E: *yiga.* (I answer her first question, and try her suggestion.) *iyusdi/h/no detsalvwisdanehv dehadel(o)/h/quasgv dagug(o)tani nahidv hol/h/tsegvi* . . . (It's not quite right, so I take time to write in the legal pad, look at and think about what's written there in syllabary. Then I say to Meli) I'm going to try it again. *iyusdi/h/no detsalvwisdanehv dehadel(o)/h/quasgv dagug(o)tani yiga nahidv hol/h/tsegvi.* (Something is still missing. In my mind I search for it, listening to the words, letting them talk to me).

M: *iyusdi/h/no detsalvwisdanehv dehadel(o)/h/quasgv dagug(o)tani yiga nahidv hol/h/tsegvi—yiga nahidv.*

E: *dagug(o)tani yiga nahidv nigalsdisgv hol/h/tsegvi.* (I say *nigalsdisgv* like a speaker says it, leaving out the vowel '*i*' after the '*l.*' That was the word the other words were trying to tell me.)

M: Ah! *nigalsdisgv hol/h/tsegvi. hawa* 'Okay.' *yiga nahidv nigalsdisgv hol/h/tsegvi.*

E: Yeah, there we go. Did that kind of ring something there?

M: *vv osda* 'Yes, it's good.'

E: So, *iyusdi/h/no detsalvwisdanehv dehadel(o)/h/quasgv dagug(o)-tani yiga nahidv nigalsdisgv hol/h/tsegvi.*

M: *gowelia* 'I'm writing it down!'

[We both laugh]

E: It's a long one. So it's kind of like 'fast' in there, you know, because when it becomes easier, whatever becomes easy you going to learn it more.

Me: Uh uh, yeah becoming.

E: Okay, let's try again. That might be the one we need. *iyusdihno detsalvwisdanehv dehadel(o)/h/quasgv dagug(o)tani yiga nahidv nigalsdisgv hol/h/tsegvi.*

M: *vv osda yigi osda elisdi* 'Yes, that would be good. That seems good.'

E: Yeah, becomes faster when it's easier, you know? So it's in English fast—it could be fast in there—it's just that in Cherokee fast is like right there when it's become easier you're going to move faster, you know?

M: Right.

E: Okay, I guess that will do it then.

M: Are we thinking about 'after you start?' Or that doesn't matter because you're talking about . . .

E: Yeah, there are two things in there. I mean, there's two sentences in there.

M: Right.

E: *halena tlesdi tsihisul(a)gotsvi.* That's a command. (I think that's what English grammar says is a command, but, to me, it's just telling you how to do it, how to succeed at it, you just start, and don't stop.) Now it's just talking. *iyusdi/h/no detsalvwisdanehv dehadel(o)/h/quasgv dagug(o)tani yiga nahidv nigalsdisgv hol/h/tsegvi.*

M: Ahh.

E: So the first one is 'start and don't stop.' And the other sentence was 'what you do after start determines how fast, how much and how well you learn.' So, that'll cover that. *dagug(o)tani*, it will determine, it will decide. *yiga*, how much of. *nahidv*, whatever it becomes easier that you understand . . . that you're understanding it.

M: Ahh.

E: Pretty close to English?

M: *osda osda elisdi* 'It's good, that seems good.'

E: See, *nahidv nigal(i)sdisgv* whatever becomes easier will cover how well and how fast and then *hol/h/tsegvi* will determine how much you're learning.

M: Uh huh. So, let me see if I have it all written down right. I'm on like my second page of paper.

[We both laugh]

M: *halena tlesdi tsihisul(a)gotsvi. iyusdi/h/no detsalvwis- danehv dehadel(o)/h/quasgv dagug(o)tani yiga nahidv nigal(i)sdisgv hol/h/tsegvi.* Is that what you have written down?

E: Say it again.

[We both laugh.]

M: The whole thing?

E: I was miles away.

M: [Meli laughs] Okay, starting with the first part that we were working on. *halena tlesdi tsihisul(a)gotsvi. iyusdi/h/no detsalvwisdanehv dehadel(o)/h/quasgv dagug(o)tani yiga nahidv nigal(i)-sdisgv hol/h/tsegvi.*

E: Um-hm, *hol/h/tsegvi* . . . (I'm thinking about the last sentence, then fine-tune one syllable in *nahidv* by stressing *hi*) . . . *yiga nahidv nigal(i)sdisgv hol/h/tsegvi.*

M: *yiga nahidv nigal(i)sdisgv hol/h/tsegvi. hawa* 'Okay.'

E: What you are understanding, what you're learning, you know?

M: Um-hum, yeah, I think that really makes sense.

E: Well, it's pretty close. Somebody's bound to say 'I would have said it this way.'

M: Well, that's the thing, everyone has their own way of saying things, but you can, you know, make yourself understood. You say it your way and someone might have a slightly different way. But, yeah, I think this makes really good sense. It's very interesting.

E: It's just a lot of thinking—can be working the brain a little bit, you know?

M: And it's sort of making a picture of it rather than trying to like get every part of what was said in English 'oh, what about this word, what about that word?' Now, you know, you sort of get the overall feeling for what it's picturing and how that makes sense in Cherokee.

E: I like that one *dagug(o)tani yiga nahidv nigal(i)sdisgv hol/h/tsegvi*, how it becomes easier, you know?

M: *vv* 'Yes,' I like that too.

E: As you're understanding it, as you're understanding, *hol/h/tsegvi*, as you're understanding something, you know?

M: *osda* 'It's good.'

E: *wado* 'Thank you,' Meli, your addition of words is good, uh huh.

M: Oh, *wado* 'thank you.' It's really interesting to think it through and, you know.

E: Yeah. Well, I guess that's good then.

M: Well, *wado* 'Thank you.'

Update

ᏏᏲ ᏂᎦᏛ *siyo nigadv,* 'Hello, all of you,' I didn't get a chance to proofread the transcript until months later. Listening to the recordings, I heard Meli say how she liked that *halena* was more personal to you, the reader. And when I came to *nigal(i)sdisgv* I wondered if *nitsal(i)sdanehv* would be a better way of saying it. *nitsal(i)sdanehv* is more personal—'how it's happening for you.' Meli and I discussed it and changed the epigraph to:

> ᎭᎴᎾ ᏞᏍᏗ ᏥᎯᏑᎳᎪᏨᎢ ᎢᏳᏍᏗᏃ ᏕᏌᎸᏫᏍᏓᏁᎲ ᏕᎭᏕᎶᏆᏍᎬ ᏓᎫᎪᏔᏂ ᏱᎦ ᎾᎯᏛ ᏂᏣᎵᏍᏓᏁᎲ ᎰᎵᏤᎬᎢ *halena tlesdi tsihisul(a)gotsvi. iyusdi/h/no desalvwisdanehv dehadel(o)/h/quasgv dagug(o)tani yiga nahidv nitsal(i)sdanehv hol/h/tsegvi.* 'Start and don't stop. What you do after start determines how fast, how much and how well you learn.' We hope it helps you. ᏩᏙ *wado,* 'Thank you.'

Note: Spoken Cherokee sometimes drops vowels. Syllabary Cherokee—the written form of Cherokee—does not drop vowels. In order to show the dropped vowels, the translation of the epigraph is written in English and phonetics. However, the syllabary version of the epigraph is given at the end.

CHAPTER TEN

Concluding Thoughts

ED FIELDS

ᏏᏲ ᏂᎦᏛ *siyo nigadv*, 'Hello, all of you,' I am glad you are here. The book is almost done and I hope it helps you.

You know, my wife, Rita, came up with the idea for this book. She brought the idea to me, and I turned it down. Oh, I had all sorts of reasons. I said, 'I wouldn't know what to write about.' So she sat down and plotted out the book. I said, 'I work full time, I don't have time to write a book.' So she suggested a co-writer who knew Cherokee to write half the book. I said, 'I'm not a writer and don't know how to write a book.' So she said, 'I will help you, I will type, I will proof-read, I will research, I will do whatever I can to help you.' And she has done those things and more to help me.

Now, you may be a first-language speaker and you, too, may have those same reasons or some other reason for not writing a book or recording an audio file or filming a video or giving a talk or some other thing that will help save the Cherokee language. Look around you, look to see if there are one or more people who are willing to help you. It is doable. We might be the last of the first-language speakers, what we leave behind will be what is used and what we let die off with us will be what is lost. Don't let it be lost.

To you who are not first-language speakers, look around, maybe there is an elder, a first-language speaker who could use your help. Maybe they don't believe they can do something. Maybe technology is foreign to them, maybe their hearing is not as good as it once was, or their eyes get tired, or their energy level may be low, maybe there are health reasons and other concerns, but simply do like my wife, Rita, did, for every problem find a solution—kindly, gently, but always forwardly.

I want to also encourage students and learners who do know some of the language, take what you have and do something good with it. Maybe you only know the syllabary, you can make picture books of it, or video, or audio, or cards or games that help people learn it. Get creative. Maybe you know some words or phrases— same thing, get creative. Maybe you know a little or a lot—get creative with it. Put it out there in the world so it can help save the language.

I know some people would rather be behind-the-scenes or I guess what they call 'support.' You are needed. Look around, find someone or some project to get behind or support, use your time and efforts to help save the language.

You know, this is going to sound kind of strange, but I didn't believe in my end of this book project, I always knew Meli's end of it would be something the students and readers would enjoy and learn from. But for my end of it, I would tell Rita 'no one is going to want to read what I have to say' and other statements like that. I just couldn't see why anyone would want to read half a book by me, let alone a chapter.

Then one day Rita said, 'Durbin isn't here any more, but you have his books on your shelf. When you open his book, how does that make you feel? And you really looked up to your university professor, Dr. Bell, but she didn't write anything that we know of, so you don't have any book by her. But imagine if you did. Imagine that her book was on your shelf right now. How would that make you feel?' Then Rita said, 'That's how your students feel about you and your book.'

Well, I didn't know if that was how they'd feel about me and my book. But I did know how I felt about Durbin and his book and how much I would also have treasured having a book by Dr. Bell. I began to see that a book, or half of one at least, might be something that some people might want.

Rita also pointed out, 'With the passing of the first-language speakers, the language is going to change. Some of the old ways of saying things will be lost. Learners will learn things that you and other first-language speakers won't exactly agree with. A book can be around a long time, hundreds of years. It can be there to teach learners now as well as in the future. It can help keep the old ways of the language intact, as well as save the language. It can do both those things. And students need help, they need help now and they'll need help in the future. Do you think doing these things are needed?'

You're reading this book, so I guess you know my reply.

If you've come this far in the book, then you've read the chapters that have come before this. And I hope you've had a chance to not only read but to do the things in the chapters to help yourself and others.

Speaking of doing, many years ago, when my mom and dad were alive, they enjoyed making several acres of gardens. They would work to clear the old stumps, remove the stones and rocks and debris. Since we lived on a hill in Oklahoma almost every time you put a hoe in the ground you hit a rock, so it was a very bone-jarring experience and very hard work they did. But they would work all day in all kinds of weather to clear that ground of any thing that might hinder their garden from growing, to get the ground ready for their garden.

Once the ground was clear, RVᏞ *edoda,* 'dad' would hitch up the team and plow all the ground for the garden with a push plow, making rows straight and as evenly placed apart as possible. Once he was finished, all those rows looked like artwork, you know? Then RᏏ ᏙᏬᏫ RVᏞ *etsi ale edoda,* 'mom and dad' would plant the seeds by hand—each seed by hand. That took time and patience. And once the seeds were in the ground, there was still work to do as every day they had to water, to weed, to protect the little growing plants.

Can you picturize it? They get up while the morning is still dark and when dawn is arriving they are already outside, working to prepare that ground, it takes many many days, and each day when the gathering dusk is closing in they are getting closer and closer to planting time and from there to watering and protecting time and from there to harvesting time. Each evening, at the end of the day, they are tired but happy and satisfied with their efforts. They know the harvest of their efforts will benefit all the family, and be shared with the community far and wide.

You too will have to prepare your ground. You'll have to remove 'stones' and 'obstacles' so that language-seeds can be planted and can take root and grow. It will have to be done, and doing so *before* you begin will make it easier for you to go forward.

I hope in Chapter One that you took the time to look and find the 'stumps, stones, obstacles'—the doubts, fears, hindrances—to you, and that you overcame them, that you have 'cleared' them and removed them from your garden so the endangered but very needed plant, the Cherokee language, can take root and grow.

And I hope that, at the end of Chapter One, you decided to start your own Cherokee language journey. Remember, you now know how to 'clear away' and 'remove' any doubts, fears, hindrances and you can do this anytime you need to throughout your Cherokee language journey.

Having decided to start your Cherokee language journey, I hope Chapter Three helped you find where and how you want to start. And that you are now along your journey—either just beginning it or further along it. I hope, too, that the tips in Chapter Three will help you.

And I hope that in Chapter Five, having seen some of the differences and similarities between the Cherokee and the English languages and having discovered that by giving yourself time and practice you can learn Cherokee, that you realize nothing can stop you. That each difference that arises can be overcome by giving yourself time and practice. That you should treat yourself fairly, being as supportive and caring of yourself as you would a well-loved friend.

I hope Chapter Seven showed you that, just like with any language, Cherokee also has rules, and once you learn the rules and do them, you can learn any language, even Cherokee. I hope the examples of the adventures you can have in translating showed you how fun and challenging-in-a-good-way it can be. And that the chapter helped you advance in your journey.

I've been speaking of the hopes that I have for you concerning the chapters I have written, I have not mentioned Meli's chapters, that is because I know her chapters will have been a big help to you. She is a very good helper. Her chapters are written very well and contain good information and helps. And some of you might even be inspired by her stepping out to talk about her learning process, the things that helped it, to document your own journey—or even collaborate with other second-language learners to document what helped each of you in your individual journeys, so that other learners can be helped too.

I hope the translation Meli and I did was of help to you. I know some of you may be thinking that *intrusive h* and vowels that get dropped and another character takes the previous vowel are "hard" or at least strange, but remember that in English there are "hard" or strange things too. Like 'use i before e except after c' and 'drop the y when adding -ing' and 'change y to i when adding -ed,' except there are exceptions to all those rules that you have to learn too. And there are more language rules in English to learn too. All languages have their own set of rules. Learn the rules of any language and you can learn that language.

So change the way you think of it. Instead of thinking that it's "hard," just think 'huh, that's the way that language is' or 'huh, that's the way that part there works' and then just accept it and go on. You did that with English. If you can learn the English language, with all its rules, you can learn another language's rules and learn that language too.

I hope that the FAQs will answer some of your questions. I know they couldn't answer them all because there was not room. And I know you'll have more questions as you walk further along your Cherokee language journey. But by reading the FAQs, you know that answers are out there, that answers can be found, and that you will find many of the answers for yourself as you research and learn from day one onward.

And so we come to this part of the book, the Concluding Thoughts. Now that you have done the previous chapters, now that you have started your journey or are walking somewhere along the way in your journey into Cherokee, sooner or later you will teach or just share what you know with others. And that will be ᎤᏍᏛ *osdv*, 'good'! When you do teach or share, always remember to find out where each learner is, to reach them at the level they are at, and bring them upward. Or as my university professor, Dr. Bell, used to say, 'You have to find out where they are at, and then you can bring them forward in their learning.' Or as Cherokee elders and my parents said it, ᏤᏣᏚᏩᏟᎮᏍᏗ ᏤᏣᏛᏟᏴᏎᏍᏗ ᏤᏣᏗᎬᏴᏎᏍᏗ *detsadasaladihesdi, detsadatliyvsesdi, detsadageyusesdi* 'you all lift one another up, you all cling to each other, you all love and care about each other.' Or another spelling and meaning, ᏤᏣᏟᎯᎠᏂᎪᏗᏍᎪᎵᏍᏗ *detsada/h/linigohisdisgesdi*, that one "word" means 'you all be strengthening one another' or 'you all build each other up and keep each other strong' (Cherokee Bible, 1 Thessalonians 11:5).

I look back at the chapters I have written, and feel it is not enough help to you. That somehow I ought to be able to do more, to make it more graspable somehow, so you can really take hold of it and do it. But I do not know how to get enough of that in the book in a way that enables you to act on it. It is a discouraging feeling. But I have tried to do my best, and I will continue to go on, to simply do my best. And perhaps, too, there are some things that I cannot do at this point. There are some things that only you can do. I know you will be doing your best too, and that gives me hope. It is good to be doing this with you. You and I doing ᏛᏕᎩ *gadugi*, 'working together,' to save the Cherokee language.

Always remember, you can learn Cherokee—just start and don't stop, what you do after start determines how fast, how much and how well you learn.

The life of the Cherokee language is in your hands. ᏯᏆᏛᎳ ᏔᎭᏍᏗᏐᏍᏗ ᎠᎴ ᏔᏣᎵᏉᎵᏎᏍᏗ ᏔᏣᎢᏒᎢ *yaquadula itsisquadisdi ale itsalihelisgesdi itsaisvi*, 'I would like for you all to succeed and enjoy your journey.'

ᏩᏙ ᎠᎴ ᏙᎾᏓᎪᎲᎢ *wado ale donadagohvi*, 'Thank you and let us, you and I, see each other again.'

—Ed

FREQUENTLY ASKED QUESTIONS

Can I Really Learn Cherokee?

Q: My health is not the best, and sometimes I can't keep up with study. Should I give up?

Ed: No. Just continue to do what you can. Your walk into the language may be slower, but that does not make it less valuable. You are still a valuable part of the community of Cherokee learners. Never give up.

Q: I'm over 60. Isn't my brain too old to really learn Cherokee?

Mary: I started taking Cherokee Nation's online classes at the age of 63. I really wanted to learn and was very excited to have the opportunity. It never once crossed my mind that I was too old. I never questioned whether or not my brain was up to it. I believe that anyone can succeed at any age if they are motivated to learn.

Q: I'm not good at languages. Can I still learn?

Ed: Yes. You don't have to be good at languages to learn, you just have to start and not stop.

Q: Is Cherokee hard to learn?

Mary: Cherokee is considered a very challenging language for

English speakers to learn. That means that it will take more time to learn than it would to learn a language like French or Spanish, which has a lot in common with English. It doesn't mean that learning Cherokee requires some specific language-learning gene that only one in a million have inherited. So, thinking of it as "hard" is not really helpful. Time plus effort will result in learning.

Q: I've read that language is best learned in childhood, and that the older you get, the harder it is to learn. Is this true?

Mary: Anyone can learn at any age. Children learn more naturally at home, surrounded by their language, but adults have some advantages over children. For example, their learning will be more focused and deliberate, since they are learning by choice. The only limiting factor would be a negative attitude. If an adult thinks they are beyond the age of learning, they will put very little into it. If, on the other hand, and adult is enthusiastic and positive about learning, there will be no limit to what can be accomplished.

Q: Is it okay to learn the language if I'm not Cherokee?

Ed: Yes. Others have learned, are learning, and will learn Cherokee.

Q: I am very excited about learning Cherokee, but I am busy with little children at home. Any ideas that could help me learn even though I'm very busy?

Ed: Collect audios and videos of spoken and sung Cherokee language, and play them. You will be able to listen sometimes to the audio and be able to see and hear some of the videos. Do not get frustrated if the children seem too noisy or seem to demand too much of your attention from learning, be patient with them and yourself and this time in your life, and just catch what you can of the audio when you can. Sing to the little children in Cherokee. If you don't have any Cherokee songs, make some up using what Cherokee words you have. If you teach the children, they can sing along too. It doesn't matter if you can sing good or not, it's about you learning Cherokee, and you'll be hearing Cherokee and tuning your brain to it. Play Cherokee language games with the little children. And when playing non-Cherokee games, find ways to bring Cherokee words, phrases and sentences into them. Have a daily self-immersion session where you speak only Cherokee. With little children around this might only be for a few seconds or minutes, but sometimes you may have longer times or you could do several sessions scattered throughout the day. You could even involve the children if you wanted by making it a game. The bonus of speaking Cherokee-only sessions is that you are using the language, which helps you learn better, and you will also be passing Cherokee on to the little children too. Basically, just think of little things you can do to put the Cherokee language in sound and sight around you, and use it. Just remember to keep an eye on the children as you learn, as little children can sometimes be very active.

Q: I don't have much time, and only want to learn some basic words and conversation. Is that okay?

Mary: Whatever you want to learn is fine. If basic words and conversation interest you, then that is what you should study. You might find that other interests open up along the way.

Q: Why should I study Cherokee if I will never be around speakers?

Ed: How do you know you will never be around speakers? In five, ten, fifteen, twenty years from now, you may find yourself around Cherokee speakers. More people are interested in learning Cherokee now than in a long time. But, even if you are not around them, why not learn for yourself? Why not learn to just help save the Cherokee language? Why not learn to be a part of a history-making movement? Someday you can look back and know that you were a history maker, you helped save the Cherokee language. Also, there will be Cherokee speakers online to interact with.

Q: I am trying hard, but other students seem to be doing better than me. What can I do to catch up?

Mary: There's no need to compare yourself to other students. You should take pride in what you have already learned, and look ahead to what you want to accomplish. You will make your own decisions about what to study and when to study, and others may be following different plans. Most importantly, learning Cherokee is not a competition. We all learn best when we learn together, sharing what we know and helping one another.

Q: I was studying Cherokee and took some classes years ago, but couldn't keep up with it. Can I start over or should I just give it up?

Mary: You can always come back to study Cherokee. Everyone has times in their lives when they must give all their attention to other matters. Other things may take precedence. Cherokee studies and other interests have to be put on the back burner for a while. That is just part of life, and it happens to all of us. The fact that you still have a desire to learn is all that matters. Most likely, you will find that there are more resources available to you than there were even a few years ago. There is a great deal of interest in the Cherokee language today, and there are more people supporting each other. Every student is valuable, and can contribute to the language in some way. So, by all means, come back and rejoin the community of language learners.

Getting Started

Q: I want to learn Cherokee. How do I get started?

Ed: The short answer is re-read Chapters One, Two, Three and Four. Chapter One and Chapter Two may help you find fears, doubts and hindrances, and overcome them. Chapter Three and Chapter Four may help you figure out where you want to learn, and that may get you started. But if you don't want to re-read those four chapters, then start with learning the syllabary. The syllabary contains the basics, the building-blocks, the foundation. Everything else rests on and depends on the syllabary. You will need to know how to pronounce and understand the syllabary sounds for hearing comprehension, communication skills and speaking. You will need to know how to read the syllabary characters for reading. And you will need to know how to write the syllabary characters for writing. You will need the syllabary all through your Cherokee language journey. If you can, get in-person instruction, that is best as that way you can hear the sounds and see how the instructor's mouth forms the sounds and you can ask questions. Next best, is a video-with-audio source as you can hear the sounds and see how the instructor's mouth forms them. If you can't get that, then third best is an audio source as you can still hear the sounds.

Q: How long will it take to learn the language?

Mary: There is no timetable that can tell you how long it will take you to learn Cherokee. Everyone learns differently, depending on their situation and their desire. The more time you have to devote to learning, and the more wisely you use that time, the more quickly you will learn. However, it's important to realize that learning doesn't always go in a straight line. There are always things that come up with family, work or other circumstances, that may slow progress from time to time. There is also no finish line to cross. I don't think any language ever has an endpoint where someone can say, 'I've done it! I know everything about this language.' I began learning in 2014, and I still have a lot to learn. In fact, I will be learning the rest of my life. So, in thinking about how much time it will take, set reasonable goals. If you set a goal to be a fluent speaker in six months, that is not a reasonable goal. But, if you decide you would like to aim for being really good at telling time in Cherokee in a month or two, you will have set a goal that can be reached. So, remember to set small goals that are attainable, and when you look back at the end of a year, you may be surprised at how much you have learned.

Q: I hear a lot about how difficult the language is. Can it also be fun?

Ed: Yes. If you're learning with in-person instruction, then your in-person instructor may be fun. If your in-person instructor is not fun, then you can still make it fun. Cherokee can be as fun as you can make it. You are in charge of how much fun it is for yourself.

Q: What should I learn first?

Mary: I think it's best to learn a few things very well. For example, you could learn numbers, then move on to telling time, and writing the day's date. Students may learn a list of numbers and think they know them well. But it is quite a different thing to call them up from memory, and to use them to tell time or to relay a phone number to someone. It is never a waste of time to work with basics. Think of these words as building blocks upon which all else will be built. These are just suggestions, but you can begin with anything that interests you.

Q: Should I memorize word lists?

Ed: Only if this works for you. If it doesn't, then find another way to learn Cherokee words. One time I was at a conference and someone asked Durbin Feeling a question about how to learn Cherokee and he replied something like 'just get a list of Cherokee nouns and a list of Cherokee verbs, and start using them.' You see, using Cherokee will help you learn it.

Q: Is there a Cherokee dictionary you would recommend?

Mary: I highly recommend the *Cherokee-English Dictionary* by Durbin Feeling and William Pulte, if you can find it in print. Additionally, there is an online dictionary which contains all the entries in the *Cherokee-English Dictionary*, plus other words from verified sources. Most students consider it one of their most treasured resources. You can access the dictionary here: https://www.cherokeedictionary.net/

Q: Why can't I find the word I want to know in the Cherokee dictionary?

Mary: Words are listed in the dictionary by the third person, present tense form. A student may see a word in a different form, with additional prefixes and suffixes and find it difficult to figure out what the third person form should be. It can be helpful to read the dictionary introductory material to better understand how the words are listed. Also, you can search by the English word if you know it. Looking up words will get easier over time as your understanding increases.

Q: What basic things do I need to learn besides speaking and writing Cherokee?

Ed: Those are good basics, and reading Cherokee is also a good basic. And since these all use the syllabary, a first basic is to learn to say, write and read the syllabary. Aim to learn the syllabary sounds so well that you can pick each sound out of the spoken language. 'Ah,' you'll say when you learn them that well, 'that word didn't have *tsi* but *ki*' or 'there was a slight *s* sound in that word.' Train your ears and your brain to the sounds. It's all about the sounds and how they are put together. Learning the syllabary sounds this well will come in handy when you begin to converse with speakers outside of the classroom.

Q: What is the most important quality that will help me learn Cherokee?

Ed: Don't stop. Or I guess that is called the quality of persistence or perseverance or plain ol' stubbornness or just being mule-headed. Remember the simple formula: Start, and don't stop.

Speaking Cherokee

Q: I don't live anywhere near Cherokee speakers. Can I still learn to speak Cherokee?

Mary: It would be ideal to live near a community of speakers, but most of us do not. We know that there are around 2000 speakers left at this time, and the reality is that sometime in the future learners may have to go forward without contact with speakers. However, that should not be discouraging. We all just have to be more resourceful in finding ways to learn. Additionally, we can improve our speaking at home by practicing with family, and by creating an environment where we see and hear Cherokee daily. For example, you can post Cherokee words and posters around your house, and listen to the Cherokee language videos or the Cherokee Nation radio show. There are online classes, books with audio, and many videos that provide examples of beautiful Cherokee speech, and we can all take advantage of those. And we can join with others to practice and improve our conversational skills.

Q: I've been studying Cherokee for a while, but I still can't understand much of the language when I hear it. Why is that?

Mary: I can empathize. I remember feeling lost when I listened to Cherokee outside of class. I had a hard time trying to pick out a single word I heard in a video. The reason is that in classes, you are presented with a controlled set of words, which are fully explained and pronounced carefully. In normal speech, word endings are often dropped, and it can be hard to hear where one word stops and another begins. Also, Cherokee has sounds that are very different from English, so we just aren't fully programmed to pick them out.

Q: How can I improve my listening?

Mary: Listening and understanding Cherokee takes time, but your efforts will be repaid. The best way I've found to improve listening is to find a very short recording of spoken Cherokee and listen to it over and over again without looking at the translation. It could be from a video, from the audio for a book, or even a recording of a class. When I say short, I mean just a few words to start. Listen to the clip over and over and write down what you hear. At first you can try this with recordings for which you have a translation. Later, you can try a recording for which you don't have a translation—just remember to keep it very short. Even if you only can pick out a sound or two, write it down. Return to it again and again and I can pretty much guarantee you will be able to catch a little more each time. If you are taking classes, get in the habit of listening with your eyes closed from time to time. There is a big difference between understanding a word while you are looking at it written down, and understanding it when hearing it only. If you do these things often your listening ability will improve rapidly.

Q: How do I find a speaker to teach me conversation?

Ed: Since I don't know where you live or anything, and since there is not enough room here, see Chapter Three as it gives pointers on finding some in-person and online ways of learning.

Q: I'm a new learner but am embarrassed to speak. What if I make a mistake and people laugh at me?

Ed: They say laughter is good medicine and helps people live longer, so you will help them live longer. And that's a good thing to do. So change your thinking to think of it like that, as a good thing. Or, to look at it another way, if they laugh at you in a mean way, they are probably not your friends nor are they supportive or even doing ᏍᏏ *gadugi,* 'working together.' So you will learn something important about them. Also, you can practice alone until you feel comfortable speaking to others. Or with your first speaking effort, phone someone. You won't see them and they won't see you. You can even wait until the end of the phone conversation to try your first speaking effort. You can say ᎥᏙᎳᎠᏎᎢ *donadagohvi,* 'let us, you and I, see each other again,' and then, if you're worried they'll laugh or if you're feeling too nervous and need to take a breather, you can end the phone call. But at least you will have started speaking Cherokee. And the next time will be less tense. Just don't put off speaking too long as it tends to get easier and easier to put off things we are afraid of. And fear when it gets in one area of you and your life to hinder or stop you, will spread into other areas of you and your life to hinder and stop you. And that is not a good thing. But if you have a good group of people, a supportive group, then you may be worrying for nothing. Fear may be trying to hold you back from doing something that will delight you and bring you joy. More than likely, once you do speak, you will find it not as scary or embarrassing as you thought.

Q: Do I have to be fluent to speak to others in Cherokee? I only know a few words, but would like to use them.

Mary: You don't have to wait until you are fluent to use the language and speak to others. If you meet someone who speaks Cherokee, say ᏏᏲ *siyo*, 'Hi!' Let them know that you are still learning. Most Cherokee speakers will be very happy to meet someone who is studying the language. They might even teach you a new word or two. You can also speak Cherokee to people you see everyday in your community. And you can find other learners in your classes or on social media who would like to practice. It can be a lot of fun and you will be helping one another to learn and to build confidence at the same time. And remember to practice speaking at home with family members, or even by speaking to yourself in the mirror. The more you use the language, the more natural speaking will become.

Q: What if I am more interested in linguistics than speaking?

Mary: Linguistic studies are very important to record details of the language which will be very helpful to future learners. Follow your heart and study what calls to you. Your interests may expand as you continue studying.

Q: How can I find out how to pronounce the words correctly?

Mary: The best way to hear correct pronunciation is to listen to a Cherokee speaker. If you have a speaker in your family or among your friends, you could ask if they have time to help. Taking a class taught by a speaker will help tremendously. This could be online or in-person. You may want to take advantage of books with audio such as *See, Say, Write*. It is also helpful to use the Word List on the Cherokee Nation's website. Many of the words have audio. You can access the site here: https://language.cherokee.org/word-list/

Q: I am thinking about moving to Tahlequah, Oklahoma so I could be around speakers everywhere I go. Wouldn't that be the best way to learn?

Ed: Unfortunately speakers would not be everywhere in Tahlequah, Oklahoma. In the past they were. And someday they will be again if we all do our part. As to the best way to learn Cherokee, the best way is the way that works for you.

Q: What if I study and study, but never learn to be fluent?

Ed: I've never heard of that happening. But even if five, eight, or ten years later (I don't know how long a time 'study and study but never learn' covers) you find it has happened, what have you lost? All that time your brain has been exercised and kept sharp, active and alive. You've met some great fellow learners, maybe even made friends. You've been part of a history making movement. You've inspired, motivated, encouraged others to learn—whether you've realized it or not—who maybe are fluent by now or who go on to be fluent. And you have learned some Cherokee. But, as I said, I've never heard of it happening. But should you find yourself studying and studying but never being fluent, remember that anywhere along the way you can adjust and fix your learning journey. If verbs are giving you trouble, you can fix that. If pronunciation is giving you trouble, you can fix that. It's all fixable. Just tailor-make the journey to fit your needs. After all, it's your journey. You're the one in the driver's seat, you're the one in charge.

Helping Children and Other Family Members Learn

Q: I want my children to learn Cherokee but I don't know enough to teach them. What can I do?

Ed: Well, I guess, two things at least. One, begin to learn Cherokee. Two, start teaching them. You don't have to learn a lot at first, just enough to start teaching them and then continue learning to stay slightly ahead of them so you can teach them. Basically you are learning and still learning while you teach them. Someday they may catch up with you, and that will be great. The other thing you could do is to find someone else to teach them, this could be an audio, video, online source or in-person learning. And you can use print sources—books, posters, etc.—too. If you can't find something in Cherokee, such as a coloring book or learning puzzle or game, then make it. You can even have your children help if you like. For instance, you could make a matching card game. You could cut out the cards, they could each draw a set of animals with the names written in Cherokee or a set of numbers written in Cherokee until all the sets are done. Then you shuffle the cards, deal them out face down, and the children take turns turning over two cards, each time they turn a card over they have to say the name in Cherokee on the card (the name of the animal or number), and when they turn over two cards that match you and they can say ᎣᏍᏛ *osdv*, 'good!' or some other Cherokee word or phrase. Just think of things you can do to teach them and don't let the lack of materials stop you. In the old days we made up our own games and created our own toys. Your children will learn Cherokee and also learn to not let hindrances stop them from achieving their goals. Cherokee Nation has coloring books and posters and such. Hopefully more and more materials will be available over time and hopefully others beside Cherokee Nation will create and make them available. But, also, a parent or teacher can create learning materials for children. Don't let any lacks or hindrances stop you or them from learning.

Q: Are there any learning materials for children?

Mary: The Cherokee Nation has created many wonderful learning materials for children which are available on their website. You will find coloring and activity books about animals, snakes, mushrooms, wild onions, cooking, as well as traditional Cherokee stories. https://language.cherokee.org/learning-materials/children-s-books/ The Cherokee Nation also has plenty of teaching materials, which can help the parent prepare to better teach their young ones: https://language.cherokee.org/learning-materials/teaching-materials/

Q: How can I get my children interested in learning Cherokee?

Ed: Make it fun for them. Remember to praise them. And love them. Even when you feel frustrated or some other negative emotion, don't let it steal from your time with them and the Cherokee language learning time with them. Don't get angry with them, or push them way beyond their ability. Also, respect their individualness. For instance, don't brag on one as a great example of what the other should be, as this will make the other feel negative about their self as well as maybe make them dislike or be bitter towards their sibling. And also, show respect and gently expect they show you respect in return. For instance, if they want to talk about something they're interested in but you have no interest in that subject, then let them talk about it and really listen to them in such a way that they know you're listening to them, even ask questions. And then when they finish or when you feel they've had enough of the floor time (which you give them), you talk about Cherokee. At first, they may not want to talk about Cherokee, but if you continue to show respect, and gently expect that they show you respect, then sooner or later they'll begin to allow you floor time and they will even really listen. I am not saying you should allow them to talk about bad things in their floor time, as parent it is up to you to correct and guide them into being the best person they can be. The world will hammer at them and try to mold them into its shape, which most probably will not be the shape Creator created them to be, so you will have to do your best to help them find their Creator-given shape. It is your love for them, and their love for you, that holds the Cherokee learning time together. Keep that love at the forefront. Keep it working for you and your children.

Q: How can I get my family members interested in learning Cherokee?

Ed: If they are babies-in-the-womb, simply speak and read aloud and sing to them in Cherokee. If they are babies outside-the-womb, again simply speak and read aloud and sing to them in Cherokee and teach them. If they are little children, make it a fun and happy time with bright colors and fun sounds—ring bells when they get correct answers, exclaim *osdv!* when they say a new word they've learned, give out gold star stickers or do high-fives or something fun for when they've surprised you or themselves with their ability to learn—just think of ways to make learning fun and interesting. If they're teenagers and/or adults, find out what interests them and bring Cherokee into it. For instance, if they like to ride their bicycles, show them video/audio or read them accounts of the Remember the Removal bicyclers. Show them the Trail of Tears route they bike. Research and find interesting things about the journey to share with them or bits of wisdom the bicyclers learned along the way. If their interest is cooking or sports or whatever, just find Cherokee things to bring into their field of interest. And while you're at it, bring in the Cherokee language, talk about the fact that it's endangered and what do they think it would feel like if the Cherokee language died or what do they think will happen to the language when the last speakers depart this world and there are no first-language speakers anymore. Sometimes it is only a lack of knowing about something, or of really thinking about it or of looking at if from their-own-personalized perspective, that will help them. So make it personal to them. Also, have honest, heartfelt conversations with them about how you want them to learn Cherokee. Explain to them why you want them to learn, and tell them what's in it for them, what do they get out of it—I'm not talking about bribing them, but pointing out to them some way that shows them Cherokee is indeed important to them. Also, they may have fears, doubts, hindrances in their way that you'll need to find out about and hopefully be able to help them overcome. But if they don't want to learn Cherokee at all, then maybe ask if they will at least learn some. If they don't want to learn even some, then ask them if they will at least help you learn. By helping you learn they will pick up some accidentally. And even if they don't want to help you learn and so they learn accidentally, you can still put Cherokee in sight and sound around your home and speak aloud, sing aloud in Cherokee and by doing so introduce them 'accidentally' to the sounds and to learning the language. Remember, you cannot force people to do things, but you can lead and guide. Let love and wisdom help you help them.

Q: If my family members don't want to learn, is it still worth it for me to learn?

Ed: Yes. For yourself but also for them. I can't tell you how many learners I've met over the years who have told me that when they were younger they had an opportunity to learn the language but turned it down and then years later—in their 20s, 30s or even 60s and 80s—they decided to learn the language in honor of their parent or loved one who spoke Cherokee all those years ago. They usually express regret that they turned down that long ago opportunity, but they're glad that they have finally come home to learning the Cherokee language. You do not know what the future holds for them. You learning now could be the thing that later brings them home to learning the Cherokee language for themselves. And then their learning the language could, in turn, be what leads some future descendant home to learning the Cherokee language too. It's a domino effect, even if slightly delayed. So, yes, it is still worth it for you to learn.

Cherokee is an Endangered Language

Q: Why is Cherokee considered an endangered language?

Mary: UNESCO has determined that when children are no longer learning a language as their first language in the home, then that language is considered definitely endangered. Since most children in Oklahoma are not learning Cherokee at home as their primary language, Cherokee falls into that category.

Q: What is language preservation?

Mary: Language preservation is the effort to keep endangered languages from dying out. Language classes for children and adults, the creation of language learning materials, and language documentation are all important parts of language preservation.

Q: How can one person help the language by learning?

Ed: One person can do a lot. Look at Sequoyah. What would the Cherokee language be today if Sequoyah had not invented his syllabary? Can you imagine a world without the syllabary? 'Well,' you might be thinking, 'I'm not Sequoyah, what help can I be?' That depends on you. You could learn the language and do a lot to help or do a little to help or do almost nothing—I cannot say 'or do nothing' next because there is no such thing here. So I say 'almost nothing,' since if you learn the Cherokee language you will do something. And you will be counted as one who learned the language—books, articles and others who count such things will count you. Also, you will be counted as one who attended a class or one who was part of the history making movement to save the Cherokee language. And you, whether you realize it or not, have people who watch what you do or know what you do. One or more of them may be inspired or encouraged by your learning the language, so that they too decide to learn it. One person can help the language by learning. But you decide how much help you'll be to the language.

Q: What does it mean when I hear people say, some families have lost the language?

Mary: If a family has lost their language, it means the language has not been passed down to the younger generations and is no longer spoken in the family. This has happened for a number of reasons. One tragic reason is that, in the past, many native children were forced into boarding schools and forbidden to speak their language. This was an attempt to separate children from their families and culture with the aim of eradicating their native way of life. Children were sometimes harshly punished for speaking their language in the boarding schools, and when they were grown, the memory of such treatment made them understandably hesitant to pass the language down to their own children. In other instances, parents who were not sent away as children, but still felt the pressure of English becoming more and more dominant around them, decided that their children would have better opportunities in life if they spoke only English. These are just two of the reasons families may have lost their language, but they need not feel they have lost the language for good. Children and grandchildren are learning Cherokee and sharing what they know with their families and communities.

Cherokee Grammar

Q: Everyone says the verbs are hard to learn. What's so hard about them?

Mary: Cherokee verbs contain a lot more information than do English verbs. For example, one verb can tell who is doing the action to whom, what the action is, and when it takes place. Many verbs can tell much more than that. Students learning Cherokee will need to open up their idea of what a verb can be. Learning little by little will help anchor your understanding of verbs, and keep you from feeling overwhelmed.

Q: What are classifying verbs in Cherokee?

Mary: Classificatory verbs are sets of verbs that use different forms according to the nature of the object being spoken about. The five categories are: living, liquid, long and rigid, flexible, and neutral. For example, if you say 'I have a piece of paper,' you would use a verb form of 'to have' that shows the object is flexible. On the other hand, if you say, 'I have a pencil,' you will need to use a form of 'to have' that shows you are talking about something long and rigid. Remember, Cherokee can be very specific. This is part of what makes it so interesting.

Q: I heard that a past tense verb can have a different ending if you weren't there to witness what happened. Can you help me understand that?

Mary: There is a past tense in Cherokee used when the speaker wasn't present to witness the action. This is called the reportative past tense, also referred to by some as the non-experienced past tense. An example of a past tense verb would be: ᎤᏩᏂᏛ *uwonisvi*, 'he or she spoke.' The past tense ending is *-vi*, which would be used if the speaker were there to witness the person who spoke. If, on the other hand, the speaker was not there, but only heard that someone spoke, the verb would be ᎤᏩᏂᏎ *uwonisei*, 'he or she reportedly spoke.' The *-ei* ending to the verb shows that the speaker was not personally present when the person spoke. You will find the reportative past tense widely used for telling traditional stories, since the storyteller is relating things from long ago that have been passed down through generations, rather than directly experienced by the storyteller.

Miscellaneous Questions

Q: What is the Master Apprenticeship program and who can apply?

Mary: The Master Apprenticeship program is a Cherokee Nation program designed to create new speakers among adults. It is currently a two-year, forty hours per week program in Tahlequah, Oklahoma. Anyone 18 and older can apply. More information can be found here: https://language.cherokee.org/language-programs/cherokee-language-master-apprentice-program/

Q: I see the same word spelled differently by different speakers. Are they making mistakes?

Ed: The way Cherokee first-language speakers spell words depends on how they learned from their family and friends. There was no school for Cherokee learners to learn how to uniformly spell or do grammar, and so on. The language was orally learned from family and friends. If you're concerned a word is a mistake, ask other speakers if it is a mistake or not.

Q: What does studying the words mean?

Mary: I can't count the number of times I've heard Ed say in class, 'Study the words!' Studying the words can mean different things to different students depending on whether they are beginners or more advanced. If you are studying the words, you are finding out whatever you can about the words. To a beginner, that might be looking up the word in the dictionary to see if there is more than one meaning, and also to carefully read the sample sentences in the dictionary entries. That way, a student can begin to understand the word in context. Another student, a bit more advanced, may begin to analyze the word, and if it is a verb, look at the verb prefix to see who is doing the action, and at the verb suffix to see when the action of the verb takes place. They might also work out how to conjugate the verb. An even more advanced student might analyze the verb more deeply, identifying all the component parts of the verb. They might also find closely related words in the dictionary and note the similarities and differences, and use the words in their own writing and speech. A student who is quite advanced, will delve more deeply, searching for examples of the words in the New Testament translated into Cherokee, *Cherokee Phoenix*, and in books like *Poor Sarah*, to find nuances of meaning. They will also note how words may have changed over time. Very advanced students might also analyze and write down the verb parts in detail, using a book like Brad Montgomery-Anderson's *Cherokee Reference Grammar* as a guide. This would help prepare a student to do translation in the future. They could also deepen their own understanding of the words by using them in their own speech and writing, reflecting any different meanings they may have found. In this way, they will have begun to understand the words in the context of Cherokee grammar, speech, writing, history and culture.

Q: What is the Cherokee Language Consortium?

Mary: The Cherokee Language Consortium holds gatherings of Cherokees from the Cherokee Nation, the United Keetoowah Band of Cherokee Indians, and the Eastern Band of Cherokee Indians. The goal is to meet quarterly to discuss creating new words and teaching materials in Cherokee.

RESOURCES

This is a list of resources that students of Cherokee might find useful. Many of them have already been mentioned in earlier chapters.

Cherokee Classes

Cherokee Nation offers free online Cherokee classes with native speaker, Ed Fields. Three levels are offered and classes meet twice a week for ten weeks. During class students view a live video feed of Ed teaching Cherokee as well as slides of the material being covered. They participate in class through a chat, answering questions Ed asks, asking their own questions and making comments. Ed explains the words and phrases and answers questions. Ed enlivens the class with drawings and sometimes stories to help to teach the Cherokee worldview. Students who successfully pass the post-test will receive a certificate of completion for the course. Registration for the course is available at: https://learn.cherokee.org

Cherokee Nation offers a free Immersion Class with Ed Fields. This is a week-long, in-person class with instruction in various topics, including useful vocabulary and greetings, and much more. Cherokee Nation also offers in-person community Cherokee classes within Cherokee Nation's fourteen-county area in Oklahoma, and also through the At-Large Cherokee communities located elsewhere in the country.

Mango Languages now offers Cherokee language lessons for free.

The lessons are intended to teach basic vocabulary, using recordings by native speakers. Cultural and grammar notes are included in each lesson, and you can record your pronunciation and match it to the speaker's pronunciation for every word. You can access the course here: https://mangolanguages.com/available-languages/cherokee/

The Cherokee Master Apprenticeship program is a two-year, full-time program for adults 18 and over to learn Cherokee. Students study in Tahlequah, Oklahoma, working with speakers and receiving instruction. Details on the program and how to apply can be found here: https://language.cherokee.org/language-programs/cherokee-language-master-apprentice-program/

Myrtle Driver Johnson's "Cherokee Textbook" is available online from The Kituwah Preservation & Education Program: https://ebcikpep.com/cherokee-language-lessons-mdj-%20textbook/?%20fbclid=IwAR3pAUCrFGz_9itDibs6w7x3Vq831vmx-brERz4ux

Classes Through Universities

Rogers State University offers prerecorded Cherokee classes taught by Wade Blevins. Stories, songs and rhymes are used to help students learn and retain vocabulary naturally. Each level consists of 48, hour-long videos. You can watch the videos on your own or enroll for a certificate program. College credit is also an option. For more information: https://rsu.tv/cherokee/

The University of North Carolina, Asheville, offers courses through their Cherokee Language Program. Class information can be accessed here: https://languagesliteratures.unca.edu/learn/curriculum/cherokee/

Western Carolina University's Cherokee language program offers courses that will count toward an undergraduate minor in Cherokee

Studies, or to fulfill foreign language requirements. More information can be found here: https://cherokeelanguage.wcu.edu/

University of Oklahoma has a Native American Language Program that offers classes in Cherokee language. More information can be found here: https://www.ou.edu/cas/nas/native-american-language-program

Northeastern State University offers a Cherokee Education B.A.ED. degree. Further information can be found here: https://catalog.nsuok.edu/content.php?catoid=32&navoid=1890

The University of Arkansas has begun offering Cherokee language courses to be taught by a native speaker. You can read about the course here: https://catalog.uark.edu/undergraduatecatalog/coursesofinstruction/chrk/

Dictionaries

Cherokee-English Dictionary by Durbin Feeling, and edited by William Pulte, was originally published in 1975. This dictionary also contains Durbin Feeling's invaluable Grammar Guide. This book is currently out-of-print, but is available as a "Log In & Borrow" book on https://archive.org/details/cherokeeenglishd0000feel/page/n5/mode/2up

Additionally, a free PDF download of the entire dictionary is available at: https://www.pdfdrive.com/cherokee-english-dictionary-e191745359.html

Cherokee-English Dictionary Online Database contains all the entries from *Cherokee-English Dictionary* by Durbin Feeling, along with Durbin Feeling's Grammar Guide. In addition, new words are continually being added from verified sources such as the

Consortium Word List, Microsoft Computer Terms, The Noquisi Word List, the Old and New Testament, and more. You can access the dictionary here: https://www.cherokeedictionary.net/

Dictionary of the Cherokee Language was compiled J.T. Alexander in 1971, using the list of words written down by Levi Gritts. This is an out-of-print book, which may come up for sale once in a while.

Raven Rock Cherokee-English Dictionary was complied by Michael Joyner and TommyLee Whitlock from material collected by Duane King in North Carolina. The book can be downloaded here: https://www.pdfdrive.com/raven-rock-cherokee-english-dictionary-e189447658.html

"Word List" from the Cherokee Nation allows you to enter a word in English or in phonetic Cherokee into a field for translation. Most of the Cherokee words will have an audio file which can be downloaded. https://language.cherokee.org/word-list/

The "Cherokee Nation Consortium Word List" is the result of collaboration among the three federally recognized Cherokee tribes, who meet regularly to discuss adding and creating new words and learning materials. The most current list is available here: https://language.cherokee.org/language-programs/cherokee-language-consortium/

Instructional Course Books

See, Say, Write is a free course available online through the Cherokee Nation. It consists of short, progressive lessons, complete with audio recorded by Durbin Feeling. The course was originally designed to teach Cherokee speakers to read and write syllabary but is very useful for anyone learning Cherokee. New syllabary characters are introduced in each lesson. There are

also activities to help students learn more effectively. https://learn.
cherokee.org/

We Are Learning Cherokee is a free online lesson book written with
the second-language learner in mind, and it introduces a number
of grammar topics. Audio is included. https://learn.cherokee.org/

Beginning Cherokee by Ruth Bradley Holmes and Betty Sharp
Smith. This is often the first textbook students come across. It
was first published in 1976 as text only, but some later editions
came with audio. The book contains 27 lessons, covering topics
like classroom phrases, the Cherokee verb, animals, relationships,
shopping and more.

Introduction to Cherokee was published by Various Indian Publishers
in 1990. It is presented in the form of a workbook and comes with
audio CDs. Narration for the audio is by Gregg Howard and lessons
were recorded by Cherokee speaker, Sam Hider. There are 22 lessons
on basic topics such as numbers, money, days of the week, food,
weather and more. There are exercises included in each chapter.

Intermediate Cherokee was published by Various Indian Publishers
in 1999. This book is designed to be a follow-up to *Introduction to
Cherokee*. It is presented in the form of a workbook and comes with
audio CDs. There are five different modules dealing with different
topics including Cherokee Culture and history, verb prefixes, sub-
ject-object pronoun prefixes, relationship words, and many other
useful subjects. The audio was recorded by Durbin Feeling and
Sam Hider.

Cherokee Language Lessons by Michael Conrad is available in a
Kindle edition, published 2020. This book shows students how
to incorporate TPR and TPRS into their language learning. TPR,
total physical response, has students perform actions in response

to commands. TPRS (teaching profociency through reading and storytelling), uses storytelling and reading to help students learn. At the beginning of the book, students are introduced to the tones and the syllabary. Vocabulary is introduced gradually from the very beginning, so the student will be learning new words and concepts at the same time. This book is suitable for the very beginner, and for anyone at any level who wishes to increase their comprehension and speaking ability. https://www.cherokeelessons.com/pdf-downloads/Cherokee-Language-Lessons-Volume-I-embedded-cover.pdf

Learning Materials have been created by Mary Rae for DAILP, The "Digital Archive of American Indian Language Preservation and Perseverance" website. These lessons are designed to help students begin working with older documents in Cherokee. Audio lessons based on the documents will help students develop important listening skills. The lessons can be accessed here: https://dailp.northeastern.edu/lessons/

"Cherokee Language Lessons" is an online site created by Michael Conrad which has a variety of learning materials including apps, books to download, lessons, stories and more. It is well worth your time to explore this site: https://www.cherokeelessons.com/

Simply Cherokee: Lets Learn Cherokee Syllabary by Marc Case was published in 2012. This is a workbook for learning syllabary and many people have had great results. It teaches by associating the shape of the characters with short stories, and it works.

Cherokee Grammar Topics

Cherokee Reference Grammar by Brad Montgomery-Anderson was published in 2015. It was originally designed for linguists, but students of Cherokee have found it very useful. The language seems quite technical at first, but if a student takes time to learn the terminology, he or she will find it a very valuable resource. The book comes with a CD which has recordings of many of the words in each chapter.

A Handbook of the Cherokee Verb by Durbin Feeling, Craig Kopris, Jordan Lachler and Charles van Tuyl was published in 2003. This book is an introduction to the verb. It explains how the verb may be broken down into its component parts, and helps the student learn how to analyze the verb. There are very useful exercises throughout. The book can be downloaded in PDF form from the Cherokee Nation website: https://language.cherokee.org/learning-materials/teaching-materials/

Cherokee Grammar Outline by Wyman Kirk is available online at Scribd.com This is a brief overview of Cherokee grammar, very helpful in giving the student an idea of how the language works. It will be necessary to sign up for the site, at least for a trial membership. https://www.scribd.com/presentation/396520773/Cherokee-Grammar-Outline-F2018-pptx

Verb Reference Book by Wyman Kirk gives detailed information about how verbs are conjugated in Cherokee. This is a great reference of conjugated verbs, and it's very easy to use. You can access it here: https://www.scribd.com/document/95229343/VRB-Didehloqwasgi-2012

Other Materials by Wyman Kirk on Scribd.com include "Cherokee Grammar Negative 'Don't' Commands," "Cherokee Grammar 'Go' Suffix," "Cherokee Grammar Dependent 'When' Clauses," "Cherokee Grammar: 'Can' and 'Cannot.'" Wyman Kirk makes complex concepts understandable with his clear, direct explanations. You can search for his work here: https://www.scribd.com/search?content_type=tops&page=1&query=Wyman%20Kirk&content_types=tops,-books,articles,documents,sheet_music,podcasts&language=1

Cherokee Verbs: Conjugation Made Easy by Prentice Robinson was published in 2004. This book contains conjugations of commonly used verbs. It is easy to use and understand. You will find it available for purchase from various online sellers.

Literature and Other Writing in Cherokee

"Digital Archive of American Indian Language Preservation and Perseverance," DAILP, is an archive of Cherokee documents which are transcribed, translated and annotated through a wide-ranging community effort. Audio for documents is recorded by native speakers. DAILP is also a language learning environment, with learning opportunities based on the documents themselves.

Cherokee Narratives: A Linguistic Study by Durbin Feeling, William Pulte and Gregory Pulte, is a collection of eighteen stories and other writings in Cherokee. Each of the writings is presented in several different ways: in syllabary, in phonetic, in English, and with word-by-word analysis. This makes the book accessible to all. Even those who have little or no understanding of Cherokee can read the English versions of the stories. Students just beginning to study the syllabary can practice their new skills, but more advanced students can study the words broken down into their component parts. This is a rare collection of contemporary Cherokee writing.

Cherokee Reader is a progressive reader for beginners in Cherokee, which introduces syllabary characters and beginning words and phrases in 84 lessons. This book may be considered a companion to *See, Say, Write*. It can be found on the Cherokee Nation website: https://language.cherokee.org/learning-materials/teaching-materials/

The Pilgrim's Progress by John Bunyan is translated in part into Cherokee. Edited by Michael Conrad. The Cherokee text appeared in the Cherokee Messenger in 1844. This is a bilingual version, and the free EBOOK is a searchable PDF. and is available here: https:// www.cherokeelessons.com/books/

Ꮎ ᎠᏓᏅᏓ ᏞᏗ ᏂᎬᎥᏍ, *The Tales of Peter Rabbit*, was translated into Cherokee by Lawrence Panther. It is available here: https://www. cherokeelessons.com/books/

Many of the children's books from the Cherokee Nation's website are helpful for beginners of any age. There are coloring books for very young students, and stories in Cherokee with English translation. Look through the offerings here: https://language.cherokee. org/learning-materials/children-s-books/

Advanced Reading

Elementary Arithmetic in Cherokee and English was published in 1870. This book has both syllabary and English translation. https://www.google.com/books/edition/Elementary_Arithmetic/ sSFHAAAAcAAJ?hl=en&gbpv=1

Poor Sarah or The Indian Woman, first published in 1833, is a translation into Cherokee of a religious tract originally written in English. The Cherokee version is thought by some to have been the work of Elias Boudinot. This book is written in syllabary only. https:// cdm.bostonathenaeum.org/digital/collection/p16057coll24/id/7/

An English version of *Poor Sarah* is available here: https:// acdc.amherst.edu/view/asc:442712/asc:442739

Cherokee Pictorial Book was published in 1888. Syllabary only. https:// collections.library.yale.edu/catalog/10927114

The Cherokee Primer was published 1854. Syllabary only. https:// collections.library.yale.edu/catalog/10927109

The Dairyman's Daughter and *Bob The Sailor Boy*, published in 1847, in syllabary only. https://collections.library.yale.edu/catalog/10927113

A version of the *The Dairyman's Daughter* in English is available here: https://ia600900.us.archive.org/8/items/dairymansdaughte00rich/dairymansdaughte00rich.pdf

Other Books of Interest

The Cherokee Syllabary: Writing the People's Perseverance by Ellen Cushman is a book for people who want to know more about the development of the Cherokee syllabary and its significance.

The Cherokee Old Testament (In Part) & Parallel Cherokee and English was published by Global Bible Society. It can be purchased on amazon.com or from other booksellers.

The Cherokee New Testament contains a treasury of Cherokee writing and thought. The text is parallel, syllabary and English. This book is available in hardback book form from the Global Bible Society. It can be purchased on amazon.com or from other booksellers.

Cherokee Language New Testament. This book uses Young's Literal Translation, which is considered to be a faithful translation from the Greek. The book can be purchased here: https://www.amazon.com/Cherokee-Language-New-Testament-English/dp/1304755029

In addition to the above resources, you can visit the authors' website: https://learningcherokee.com

NOTES

STEPPING ONTO THE PATH

1. "Atlas of the World's Languages in Danger." http://www.unesco.org/languages-atlas.

2. Ellen Cushman. *Cherokee Syllabary: Writing the People's Perseverance* (Norman: Univ Of Oklahoma Press, 2013), 197.

IF I CAN LEARN, SO CAN YOU

1. William C. Woodbridge, Ed., *American Annals of Education and Instruction, For the Year 1832*, Vol II. (Boston: Allen and Ticknor, 1832), 184. https://archive.org/details/americanannalsof02edit/page/n231/mode/2up.

2. Marc W. Case, *Simply Cherokee: Let'sLearn Cherokee Syllabary* (Bloomington, IN: AuthorHouse, 2012).

3. Durbin Feeling and William Pulte, *Cherokee-English Dictionary* / Ed. by William Pulte; in Collaboration with Agnes Cowen. S.l. (Cherokee Nation of Oklahoma, 1975), 37.

4. *Digital Archive of Indigenous Language Persistence*, https://dailp.northeastern.edu/collections/dollie-duncan-letters.

MAKING FRIENDS WITH VERBS

1. Durbin Feeling and William Pulte, "Outline of Cherokee Grammar" in *Cherokee-English Dictionary* (Tahlequah, Oklahoma: Cherokee Nation of Oklahoma, 1975), 241.

1. Anna Gritts and Jack Frederick Kilpatrick, *The Shadow of Sequoyah: Social Documents of the Cherokees, 1862-1964.* (Norman Oklahoma: Univ. of Oklahoma Press, 1965), 9-10.

2. DigitalNativeMaker, "Peanutbutterandjelly.mov," Features Bonnie Kirk, YouTube, 4 January 2012, video, https://www.youtube.com/watch?v=guXgEHVuFkY.

3. J. T. Alexander, Comp., *A Dictionary of the Cherokee Indian Language*, 1971, 236.

4. Brad Montgomery-Anderson, *Cherokee Reference Grammar* (Norman: University of Oklahoma Press, 2015), 323.

5. *Tsalagi Itse Kanohedv Datlohidv Tsutsosawati Tsalagi Ale Yonega=The Cherokee New Testament, Parallel Cherokee & English: Translation Based upon the Received Text.* (Asheville North Carolina: Global Bible Society, 2015).

6. Alex Smith, "Inside the Collections." National Parks Service. U.S. Department of the Interior. https://www.nps.gov/articles/000/inside-the-collections-hocu-6262.htm.

7. *Digital Archive of Indigenous Language Persistence,* accessed September 2022, https://dailp.northeastern.edu/documents/dd9.

8. E. Boudinot, *Poor Sarah or The Indian Woman*, accessed October 2022, page 9, https://cdm.bostonathenaeum.org/digital/collection/p16057coll24/id/7/.

9. E. Boudinot, *Poor Sarah or The Indian Woman*, accessed October 2022, page 3, https://cdm.bostonathenaeum.org/digital/collection/p16057coll24/id/7/.

10. *The Cherokee Old Testament (in Part): Parallel Cherokee and English.* (Asheville North Carolina: Global Bible Society, 2016).

11. Durbin Feeling and William Pulte, *Cherokee-English Dictionary* / Ed. by William Pulte; in Collaboration with Agnes Cowen. S.l. (Cherokee Nation of Oklahoma, 1975).

12. "Noquisi Degasehiha," accessed November 2022, https://youtu.be/5xfmL1QQkaQ.

BIBLIOGRAPHY

Alexander, J. T. Comp. *A Dictionary of the Cherokee Indian Language. 1971.*

"Atlas of the World's Languages in Danger." Accessed January 3, 2022. https://www.unesco.org/languages-atlas.

Boudinot, E. (n.d.). *Poor Sarah or The Indian Woman.* Retrieved October 2022, from https://cdm.bostonathenaeum.org/digital/collection/p16057coll24/id/7/.

Case, Marc W. *Simply Cherokee: Let's Learn Cherokee Syllabary.* AuthorHouse, 2012.

Cherokee Old Testament (in Part): Parallel Cherokee and English. Ashville, North Carolina: Global Bible Society, 2016.

Cushman, Ellen. *Cherokee Syllabary: Writing the People's Perseverance.* Norman, Oklahoma: Univ Of Oklahoma Press, 2013.

Digital Archive of Indigenous Language Persistence. https://dailp.northeastern.edu/

DigitalNativeMaker. "Peanutbutterandjelly.mov." Features Bonnie Kirk. YouTube, 4 January 2012. Video, 4:41. https://www.youtube.com/watch?v=guXgEHVuFkY.

Feeling, Durbin, and William Pulte. *Cherokee-English Dictionary / Ed. by William Pulte ; in Collaboration with Agnes Cowen.* S.l.: Cherokee Nation of Oklahoma, 1975.

Feeling, Durbin, and William Pulte. "Outline of Cherokee Grammar." Essay. In *Cherokee-English Dictionary /* Ed. by William Pulte;

in Collaboration with Agnes Cowen, 241. S.l.: Cherokee Nation of Oklahoma, 1975.

Kilpatrick, Anna Gritts, and Jack Frederick. *The Shadow of Sequoyah: Social Documents of the Cherokees, 1862–1964.* Norman, Oklahoma: Univ. of Oklahoma Press, 1965.

Montgomery-Anderson, Brad. *Cherokee Reference Grammar.* Norman: University of Oklahoma Press, 2015.

"Noquisi Degasehiha." (2020). YouTube. Retrieved November 23, 2022, from https://youtu.be/5xfmL1QQkaQ.

Smith, Alex. "Inside the Collections." National Parks Service. U.S. Department of the Interior. Accessed January 7, 2022. https://www.nps.gov/articles/000/inside-the-collections-hocu-6262.htm.

Tsalagi Itse Kanohedv Datlohidv Tsutsosawati Tsalagi Ale Yonega = The Cherokee New Testament, Parallel Cherokee & English: Translation Based upon the Received Text. Asheville, North Carolina: Global Bible Society, 2015.

Woodbridge, William C., Ed. *American Annals of Education and Instruction, For the Year 1832,* Vol II. Boston: Allen and Ticknor, 1832, page 184. https://archive.org/details/americanannalsof02edit/page/n231/mode/2up